The Queen's Garden Party

Presented by

Terry Godwin

Preface

Another book of rhyming poetry which seems to go well with my readers.

This time I have been able to put my visit to the Queen's Garden Party into this collection. Naturally I was delighted to have been invited to this very special occasion for work done in promoting poetry in the Medway Towns.

I have now moved to Brighton and live with my son and family.

My poems for those who know me are often romantic, many tilted towards finding happiness and attaching poems of life and humour. I still ask for short stories that can be turned into verse. I am lucky I have a steady supply of clean jokes sent to me by readers and friends which are always greatly appreciated.

I hope my latest selection of poems with their variety will give you a laugh,

relax you, and give you a good read.

I now have my own site on face book, writer's internet, and books published by kindle.

Enjoy reading.

Terry Godwin

The Laughing Poet

1.   A Guardian Angel Smiled On Them
2.   Lucky You
3.   A Beauty of Nature
4.   About Life
5.   Beautiful Ladies
6.   Blowing In The Wind
7.   Did Fate Mean It To Be?
8.   Falling Leaves
9.   For Your Tomorrow We Gave Our Today
10.   A Woman At War Remembers
11.   Have You Seen An Angel?
12.   Autumn
13.   Procrastination
14.   To Dream Or Not To Dream
15.   Would You Like A Dance?
16.   A Bridge Of Dreams
17.   The Singing Frog
18.   Cougars
19.   Crocuses
20.   The Queen's Garden Party
21.   Pusey's Prospects
22.   The Dating Game
23.   Our Trees
24.   The Twin Towers Disaster or A True Friend
25.   How To Master A Disaster
26.   Love, Life And Happiness
27.   I Am A Woman
28.   I Hear The Silence
29.   I Remember The Lamplighter
30.   When I Knew I Was In Love
31.   Your Destiny

32.   **A Great Decision**

33.   **Golden Thoughts**

34.   **A Maiden's Prayer or That Magical Glance**

35.   **Farewell Common sense**

36.   **Goodbye Dad, Goodbye**

37.   **The Power Of Happiness**

38.   **Be Mine, Be Mine**

39.   **English Ritual**

40.   **The Silence of Peace**

41.   **A Summer Sky**

42.   **Is There A Heaven?**

43.   **A Wonderful Moment**

44.   **Sky High Generosity**

45.   **Her Great Day**

46.   **I Made A Mistake**

47.   **Maria Got What She Wanted**

48.   **I Want To Be Wanted**

49.   **Just A Thought**

50.   **Over The Hills And Far Away**

51.   **Country Ways**

52.   **A Fiddler Came To Play**

53.   **Don't Criticize**

54.   **I Thought Love Had Passed Me By**

55.   **Did They Touch?**

56.   **Reaching Out For Love**

57.   **The Price Of Freedom**

58.   **Philosophy!!!**

59.   **Enjoy It Today, Be Damned Tomorrow**

60.   **How To Be Successful In Life**

61.   **The Way It Used To Be**

62.   **God For A Day**

63.   The Ticking Clock

64.   I Am What I Am

65.   Wet Feet ---- My Treat

66.   Who Has Seen The Wind?

67.   What A Night That Was!

68.   Why Do I Cry?

69.   A Piece of Heaven

70.   A Soldier returns to Wootton Bassett

71.   A Time Will Come

72.   Change

73.   An Apple Scrump To Remember

74.   He Gave His All

75.   Singing In The Rain

76.   A Single Rose

77.   A Little Reminder

78.   A Miscellany Of Short Verse

79.   Blackberry Picking

80.   The Maid Wants A Rise

81.   Birds

82.   Blessed Peace

83.   A Lost Friend

84.   I Want To Touch The Sky

85.   It Is Wrong To Be Right

86.   If Music Be The Food Of Love, Play On

87.   Kindness

88.   A Beautiful Rose

89.   Bleep, Bleep, Bleep

90.   Birds In Summer

91.   Do All The Good You Can

92.   A Second Chance

93.   The Power Of Love

94.   Do Not Cry For Me

95.   Enjoy The Rest Of Your Life

96.   Have We Been There Before, I Think not?

97.   Going Home, Going Home

98.   The Master's Touch

99.   He Was Positive??

100.   The Wooden Bowl and Plate

101.   I Love To Walk

102.   Dad Please

103.   Thank You And Well Done

104.   A Phone Call Away

105.   My Best Friend

106.   Butterflies

107.   I Am A Warrior

108.   I Believe

109.   A Bottle Of Wine

110.   I Look Into His Eyes

111.   I Remember The Storm

112.   Do It Today, Tomorrow We Die

113.   Don't Cry For Me

114.   I Am Just A Man

115.   Alone in The Dark

116.   The Jewel In The Crown

117.   I Look At The Stars

118.   You Cannot Please Everyone All The Time

119.   Grannies Advice

120.   Goodbye My Love

121.   Mr. Nobody

122.   The Top Of The Hill

123.   The Waterfall

124.	Volunteering Can Be Good For You
125.	Does He Know?
126.	Plain Jane
127.	The Amazing Dog
128.	Make Believe
129.	Notices And Signs That Give You A Laugh
130.	Always A Treat
131.	Love And Kindness
132.	Two Kittens From Where?
133.	When Love Walks In
134.	The Wise Man Said...
135.	He Loves Me True
136.	It Didn't Seem Fair
137.	New Aspirations
138.	Mutton Dressed As Lamb!
139.	Now We Must Part...
140.	An Unpleasant Customer
141.	What A Surprise!!
142.	How To Write A Short Story
143.	Pull The Other Leg
144.	I Made It
145.	Our Wonderful World
146.	The Alphabet Of Love
147.	The Woman Of The Street
148.	The Fantasy Wife
149.	Today Will Not Come Again
150.	Passion
151.	I'm In Paradise
152.	Global Warming Is Here
153.	Our Wonderful trees
154.	Harvest Time
155.	Howzat!
156.	How To keep A Marriage Happy

1. A Guardian Angel Smiled On Them

The weather was foul, it was night of the storm,
The wind blew fierce, well above the norm.
Mary was driving down Highway One- One- Nine,
Her two boys in the back, all was quiet and fine.

Suddenly Mary's car was in a tremendous crash.
It happened so quickly, as quickly as a flash.
Mary was knocked out, when she came too,
She was jammed in and did not know what to do.

There were cars and lorries smashed up everywhere,
Calls for help, so many in agony and despair.
Over a hundred vehicles were in this terrible pile up,
That night death would drink from a full cup.

A police cop smashed the driver's glass window in,
Shouted to Mary to stay calm and we will win.
Mary Screamed "How are my boys in the back,
Save them first", with all the power she could pack.

The rescuers looked and saw no one there,
They told Mary and she was in despair.
It took half an hour to cut her out,
When out, she went charging about.

Screaming "where are my boys they must be about"
"Help me, help me" was all she could shout.
A police cop grabbed her, told her to be calm,
Her ranting and raving was causing much alarm.

She shouted "I'm looking for my two boys both dressed in a brown suit,"
The cop said "they are both in my car looking rather cute."
She rushed to the car where the boys smiled back at her,
Mary cuddled them and asked "How did this occur?"

The cop replied "Their dad handed them over to me,
I put them in the car, the best place I think you will agree.
When I was putting them in he seemed to vanish, don't know how.
I have been looking for him since, no joy, then or now."

Mary said "You will not find him, he died two years ago,
On his deathbed he promised to love us and never let go.
When we are in trouble I feel his presence is with us,
Knowing he is there is always a big plus."

Next day when the cop was writing his report on accident Highway One-
One Nine,
He wrote only a miracle could have saved them, or on that night their
Guardian Angel did shine.
Mary knew on that night it was incredible that her and her family did
Survive,
She felt blessed and would do the best for her boys while they were alive.

2. Lucky You

Lucky you, you have the future ahead, full of possibilities,
Think positive, take advantage of those opportunities.
A new day, a new beginning, fresh aims, reinvent yourself,
Make your dreams and Ideas a reality taking them off the shelf.
Look at the big horizon, strive for greater things,
Don't hold back, let your ambition fly free and soar on wings.
Become a man of vision and action, show the world what you can do.
It is you alone thinking positive, who can make your dreams come true.

3. A Beauty Of Nature

The morning dew and the bright dawn light,
Creating a spectre of brilliance and delight.
The fine interlacing is a work of intricate art,
Spun so delicately, it is perfection from the start.

When the dew has dried out, you will not see,
This framework, that is should be.
This web has woven to catch the fly,
When it flies into it, it is stuck, and doomed to die.

The spider takes his victim back to his nest,
Sucks it dry, and discards the rest.
Mother Nature decrees every creature has the right to survive,
They must kill in order to stay alive.

A spider's web is woven so quickly and with such skill,
Some regard it as beautiful, others, a death trap to kill.
Beauty and death are often entwined together,
This is the way of the world, and will be forever and ever.

4. About Life

Happiness in your heart keeps you sweet,
With a smile your neighbour and the world greet.
Trials will keep you alert and strong,
Overcome them and make the world feel you belong.

Sorrow sometime, somewhere will come to us all,
Pay respect, think of others and walk tall.
Failures will keep you humble,
The prouder you become the harder you tumble.

Success will drive you on and keep your ego glowing,
Take it in your stride, keep your energy flowing.
It is the spirit of life that will see you through,
Be positive, be kind, love your neighbour, and the world will love you.

5   Beautiful Ladies

That ladies are beautiful is a blessing to mankind,
Sometimes of course it can drive a man out of his mind.
To capture the ladies heart is man's desire,
To satisfy the needs of his sexual desire.

It is in the ladies genes to attract her men,
To win his love any way she can.
When she sees her prospect, she starts with a smile,
Her sweet talk and female charm is always there to beguile.

The art of courtship is to let the man lead the way,
Until they are bonded man can have his say,
When united, her word gently carries the day.
That's the way Mother Nature planned it so they say!

6   Blowing In The Wind

I stand alone on the cliff top,
Enjoying the suns warm glow,
And the gentle breeze,
Making my hair flow.
I watch the horizon,
Waiting for my ship to come home,

Bringing back our sailor men,
To wives, families and lovers.
The ship I seek is long overdue,
Our community is getting restless and tense,
Worry is fermenting.
A score of men, healthy and strong,
Are desperately awaited,
By their loved ones to whom they belong.

My vigil is for my groom,
On his return we will be married.
All sailors' wives live on edge,
When their soul mate is sailing the sea.
The salt of the ocean is in their blood,
He cannot endure a long stay on land.

Being land bound he cannot stand.
All sailors' wives with reluctance concede,
Their men must travel the world,
To satisfy their wayfaring need.
Nothing moves, the skyline is clear,
The sun sets, the night draws near.

I walk down the steep rocky path,
And report no sails in sight.
Another night to be suffered alone with fear,
Worrying about our loved ones most dear.
The night passes, we long for the dawn of day,
Religious or not we all pray.

The new day is here, our vigil is renewed,
Will this day answer our prayers with joy?
This is not to be so, we despair.
Children are coming to realise,
Dad might not come home again,
Hear their cries, a miserable refrain.

Two days later our ship of hope is in the dock.
The whole community down to the harbour,
With elation, with relief, with tears do flock.
The men are hungry, weary and in good spirit,
To be home again, to feel the warmth of love.

To be a sailor's wife, they must know and care,
When her man's away can be a nightmare.
Thank god we have men, who must travel the sea,
And women folk who love them and their family.

7 Did Fate Mean It To Be?

Did fate mean it to be?
If so why was he so good to me?
In this I am nothing special I can assure you,
I have done good and bad things like we all do.
My job was lowly paid and boring too,
Life was pointless until I met you.

Yes I was looking for a pretty girl,
Not expecting to fall in love with you my pearl.
I have often read that love sweeps you away,
Rhyme, reason and logic have no say.
I first saw you across a crowded room,
I was taken aback, my heart went boom, boom.

An hour later I met you face to face,
I wanted to kiss you, my arm to embrace.
I was over the moon when you agreed a date,
I did not realise it had been planned by fate.
That night I walked home full of fire and thought,
I must prove myself it for me and you to be caught.

There was work around, it wasn't hard,
Enthusiasm, youth, willing to learn was a trump card.
I got another job, rewarded me with double my present pay,
Bought some new clothes, I was on the up and up some would say.
Our courting was such great joy for me,
When we touched and kissed it made me as happy as can be.

A year on from meeting in that crowded room,
I walked down the aisle with you, my heart was still going boom, boom.
Ten years on we are blessed with a wonderful family,
I am so grateful that fate decided who my love would be.
It taught me to think positive, there is always something wonderful out
there.
When it comes, value it and treat it with great and loving care.

8 Falling Leaves

Autumn leaves falling quickly on the ground,
Winter winds blow them round and round.
Heavy rains fall making everything wet,
Black clouds blot out a depressed sunset.

Puddles created by the showers are everywhere,
Walking without cover one does not dare.
Soon the winds will blow icy cold,
Wrap up warm, don't let the bitter weather take hold.

It is good to get home and enjoy the home side fire,
To suffer the winter weather we have no desire.
It is at night time I enjoy going to my bed,
To dream of summers that lay ahead.

The leaves have now settled into a soggy pile,
They will nourish the earth, by spring vanish in style.
Autumn leaves falling quickly to the ground,
The trees will now sleep till spring again comes around.

9 For Your Tomorrow We Gave Our Today

The front line was full of gunfire from either side,
Never expose yourself or you would be on your death ride.
It has been like this for over a week,
No peace or mercy do either side seek.
Our platoon is now taking some time off to rest,
To refurbish our energies, in order to fight again at our best.

We write home to our loved ones, let them know we are alive,
Must not tell them of our success, how hard we strive.
Must not tell them we have just lost another seven men,
They died for their country, have said their last amen.
We don' know the tally of the wounded and the dying,
We are encouraged to think positive and keep trying, trying, trying.

We think of our loves ones and miss our home,
In spite of the bonhomie of our comrades we share our fears alone.
We clean and check our equipment to pass the time,
We enjoy hot fresh food not available in the front line.
We avidly seek our post praying we are not the forgotten man,
That the news is good, absence makes the heart grow fonder you
understand.

Our days of respite passed so very fast,
We pray our next fight won't be our last.
We wonder whether we would rather be killed or maimed for life,
With the latter you will be so dependent on family and wife.
They say where there is life there is hope,
I just wonder whether I could happily cope.

I have written my letters to loved ones and put them in the post,
Thinking of my small sons success, of that to my comrades I boast.
I am putting my head down for some precious sleep,
For tomorrow I have an appointment with the enemy to keep.
I often reflect on that famous quotation read out over the soldier's grave,
"When you go home, tell them of us and say,
For your tomorrow we gave our today."

When I go home I shall walk tall, with the grace of God, having done my duty,
and supported my comrades and remained brave.

10 A Woman At War Remembers

The day is nearly over, our two boys are in bed,
It's long and lonely nights I dread.
Bob, my husband is away fighting in the war,
I wonder if I will ever see him again walking through our door.
He is a commando, one of the best,
When he fights, he fights with courage and zest.
That's fine for the generals in command,
If Bob is injured or killed it's my family on remand.

Down the road there is a widow who lives on her own,
Her husband was a fighter pilot, his last aerial combat has flown.
On the mantelpiece is a photo of their wedding day,
With three medals for bravery on display.
Her love and hope for the future has been blown away.
In the war time to seek another love is difficult when everything is in
disarray.
If I lost Bob I would have to struggle for my family,
To ensure them a future, to try and make them happy.

Letters from Bob were few and far between,
Everyone precious, telling me he was still on the world scene.
I longed for his love and support both day and night,
When I went to bed, all I wanted was to see dawn's light.
The newspapers and wireless indicated we were beginning to beat the Hun,
Casualties were high, waiting to hear if your man was killed was no fun.
It was to be another year before Bob returned to my arms,
Then I could sleep without fear or qualms.
I never went to war to face the enemy's gun,
But as a mother and wife at home, worrying till the war was won,
Grateful another day passed with no harm done.
I prayed when the enemy bombers flew over our sky,
When they dropped their bombs we would not die.
Peace has come, Bob and I and the boys are together again,
Will I ever forget the time when courage and chance decided whether you
lived or would be slain?
The generations who have lived and suffered through war, women or man,
Will always remember the day when the horror of the war began.

11 Have You Seen An Angel?

I sit down and wonder what an angel is, he or she?
I have heard about them from the bible you see.
I hear they are kind and give wise advice,
They only do things that are good or nice.

They are always on hand in times of need,
They support and encourage you to succeed.
You always see them with a smiling and welcoming face,
You can be sure always of their warm embrace.

Some say only in heaven angels you will find,
If I say that is not true, don't think I am out of my mind.
I have an angel I love and see every day,
I hope my wife and I will remain together forever I pray.

12 Autumn

The summer days are fading fast,
Smiling autumn now plays its cast.
I sit under my fully laden apple tree,
In the balmy sunshine, a delightful pleasantry.
Tomorrow we shall pick up the apple crop,
If we do not they will surely drop.
In the late summer and autumn yield,
The worlds harvest from tree and field.
The harvest is collected and carefully stored away,
To feed us all some future day.
When harvests are good we celebrate the 'Harvest festival',
Many celebrate with their annual carnival.
Autumn, season of mellow fruitfulness,
Is the season that gives me great contentment and bliss?

13 Procrastinations

Procrastinations is the thief of time,
In our lives we hear so often that discouraging line.
We dither, we dally, and we hang about,
Can't make a decision, element of doubt.
The man who wins is the man who will dare,
He moves ahead, and plans with care.

In relationship to Father Time our lives are so short,
To use time wisely we should all be taught.
If we did not waste our time, the world would be a better place,
We would improve ourselves and the human race.
If we put more effort into our work and play,
Both you and I would enjoy a happier day.

Tomorrow never comes, get it done now,
When you are finished, stand back and take a bow.
What you want to do, do it this day,
It is possible another chance will not come your way.
When you have read this advice, look at yourself,
Are you going to act now, or remain on the shelf?

Procrastination is not born into you, that's true,
It's your spirit and determination that will make a new man of you.

14 To Dream Or Not To Dream

I went to see my doctor yesterday,
To ask him about my dreams per say.
I have an alternative dream each night,
They cause me worry and fright.
On the first night I can dream I am in a wigwam,
All I can see is a fierce Indian man.
In the second night I am in a tepee,
Again that Indian man is all I can see.
Doctor, please explain to me, these dreams do not make sense."
The Doctor replied "Don't worry, it just means you are too tense."

15 Would You Like A Dance?

A month ago I had never met him,
A month ago I went to dance on a whim.
That's where I saw him, he stole my heart away,
Please God, make him notice me I did pray.
His eyes twinkled with a smile I could not resist,
This man, I wanted to be his dearest.

I am not a novice at the loving game,
That I love men gives me no shame.
A woman must find what her man is all about?
Is he mean, kind, selfish, she should find out.
Is he willing to only love you, he will surely say yes,
Will he be true to you is anyone's guess.

I know I fancied him, I fancied him like hell,
Will he fancy me, only time will tell?
Now I must go in and attract his attention with female guile,
And pray he will cast on me his captivating smile.
The music for a dance does begin,
I march boldly up and ask for a dance with him.

I told him I hear he dances very well,
He is taken aback by my forwardness I can tell.
I said "My name is Jenny, I feel rhythm in my feet,
To dance with you will make my evening complete."
He replied "My name is Tony, your invitation I accept,
To miss a chance to dance with such a beautiful lady I would regret."

I warmed to his charm as any woman would,
I let him take charge, I became demur, attentive and good.
After six dances he said "It is about time I think,
To sit down and buy you a drink"
We sat down at a small table for two,
We talked and danced the whole evening through.

I was dancing on air, I was happy as can be,
I felt I had met Mr Right you see.
He asked me when the evening was nearly through,
If we could meet again? I said "Yes," wouldn't you?
Then he told me in two days time he had to go,
To America for four weeks, that was a blow.

He said he would ring me every weekend,
On that I could be sure and depend.
He took me home in his car and kissed me goodbye,
I went into my flat alone, not knowing whether to laugh or cry.
Every Sunday morning and ten o'clock spot on,
We spoke for thirty minutes, and then he was gone.

Then for a whole week the time did drag by,
I was beginning to feel without him I would die.
The month passed, back to England he came,
He didn't visit me, he said his company was to blame.
He had to be debriefed, three days it did take,
Meantime he sent me flowers, a promise he did make.

After his debriefing he would get ten days holiday,
Asked me if he could spend the time with me? What did I say?
I said that would be heavenly in every way.
I wanted him in my arms come what may.
If absence makes the heart grow fonder, this was a case,
It showed when he rang the doorbell and we came face to face.

We both smiled cautiously, kissed and gave each other a huge embrace,
We both exploded with passion and to my bedroom we did race.
This was to be a week in my life I will never forget,
Asking Tony for a dance I would never regret.
Yes we made love all week through and my heart did sing,
Before going back to his home he gave me an engagement ring.

Tony and I have two daughters who will soon be looking for a man,
Finding Mr Right is essential for every woman.
Going up to a stranger and asking him for a dance,
Because you fancy him is certainly taking a chance.
Still when you are in love you don't reason why,
When you see the man you fancy, to win him you will try.

I know I was lucky, fate was good to me,
History shows that this approach can be risky you see.
I will tell my daughters to travel slowly and take care,
When they fall in love, don't tempt fate and dare.
Still the young are headstrong and will do what they want to do,
We pray the outcome will be a good one when they see it through.

Young women in love will often only see good,
Ignore bad omens and signs when they should.
That has happened since the world began,
When women have wanted love from a man.

16 A Bridge Of Dreams

There must always be a bridge of hope,
For those unfortunates who cannot cope.
There must be a path to a better life,
Where happiness is key, not trouble and strife.

We all need a goal in life to aim for,
To satisfy our ego, to push open the door.
To a land where misery and pain is banished,
Where joy, good health and happiness is lavished.

To enjoy life there must be love, security and hope,
With these three as partners we would all elope.
It can be a hard world we all have to face,
We must try to cross our bridge of dreams to find a better place.

17 The Singing Frog

The man walked into the pub and then,
Stands at the bar and says "Something special to show you gentleman."
He opened a suitcase and pulled out a mouse,
"Would you like him to play the piano and entertain this house?"

The bar visitors said "Yes" and gave a cheer,
They all liked cheerful music with their beer.
The mouse played the piano for half an hour,
The man said "Would you like to hear a frog who can sing with gusto
And power?"

The audience cheered and said they were game for anything,
The frog sang magnificently, a joy to hear him sing.
The mouse playing, the frog singing, everyone was enjoying a great beer,
All having a great time that was clear.

Suddenly up jumped a customer who offered to buy the frog,
For five thousand pounds, which made the on-lookers agog?
The frog's owner said "okay" and took the cash,
The buyer put the frog in his bag and then away did dash.

The publican said "Five thousand pounds for a singing frog worth millions.
Wasn't your price rather modest?"
The man smiled and slowly said "Not really, you see the mouse
Is a ventriloquist."

18 Cougars

When reading an article in the Daily Telegraph magazine 'Stella,' I spotted
An article called 'Cougars'. The name here refers to older women who
Want short term relationships with young men, usually ten to fifteen years
Younger than themselves for sex and companionship with no ties for a short
Period, say for a year, and then seek another lover.

It is usually older men who want the company of younger women, it seems
The ladies are playing the men at their own game.

I have never heard of this word before used in this context, so I thought
I would educate those like me, and I was inspired to write the following
poem.

The Cougar Woman

Next week I shall be young and flirty fifty five,
I am now single and feel very much alive.
I run my own business which is doing very well,
It is in London I live, close to the sound of the Bow Bell.
I have a nice flat near the Houses of Parliament,
Which I use for my home and my gentleman's entertainment.
I proudly admit that I love to be loved, enjoy my passion too.
I enjoy being a woman especially when the man wants to woo.

"Young men" I hear you rather surprised and disbelievingly say,
Yes it is in a young man's arms where I wish to lay.
When I was forty my husband fell in love with another,
We divorced, I got a good settlement, he was useless as a lover.
With my cash I contacted a business consultant,
To set up business for me so I could be independent.
My consultant Ted was good looking, single and thirty.
I fancied him, decided to attract him by being flirty.

He responded, he too wanted sex and companionship,
We met three times a week when into my loving cup he would dip.
This relationship lasted a year, he had to move up north,
To find his replacement I now had to set forth.
I had decided I wanted another man younger than me,
He would have more drive and energy in bed you see.
Men older try to patronise and take over our association,
I don't want to be saddled with their problems and frustration.

Young men appreciate my figure and feminine guile,
Enjoy my experience and always have a welcoming smile.
Neither of us want a permanent relationship,
Just to enjoy sex and each other's loving companionship.
I have to go to my business every day,
It's weekend and evenings when we love and play.
I do prefer a man who can well and truly dance,
If he can, that makes our relationship buzz and enhance.

When I am alone and seeking a new playmate,
I become as nervous as a filly on her first date.
I dress to the nines, not a thing out of place,
Showing plenty of cleavage, short skirt, a smiling face.
Then I sit alone at my favourite bar and have a drink,
Guessing what the interested parties eyeing me do think.
It is only when the right young man asks to join me,
Do I respond with my charm and femininity.

Yes I admit I am willing to enjoy sex for just a night,
It is a way of sussing out if he is Mr Right.
It usually takes a month to find a man I desire,
With whom I wish to enjoy his company and passionate fire.
If I feel my lover is seeking a permanent relationship,
Then I will discourage him and close our partnership.
I have lived this way for fifteen years and will continue as long as I can,
I will keep on this path as long as I can attract the younger man.

I hear society brands me a cougar, a temptress on the night,
Preying on young men with my offer of sexual delight.
I don't care what society thinks, I enjoy my life, other ladies do this too,
It is my lovers choice if he wished to love me and woo.
Why should it be men only who take this stance in life,
When fed up, divorce and set up again with a new young wife.
I know I take a chance of being hurt in the life that I lead,
That alone is a thrill and I admit I do not always succeed.

19 Crocuses

A gentle sun calls "Wake up to spring,
It is time for your awakening."
Little heads appear, peeping through the earth,
Gently waving, eager to share the suns mirth.

They hide from the March winds chilly blow,
Hoping there will not be any seasonal snow.
The sun encourages them to stand up proud,
Displaying themselves as a purple cloud.

These little flowers do not bloom for long,
Long enough to sing their spring song.
Long enough to tell us spring is about,
They herald in spring there is no doubt.

20 The Queen's Garden Party

This poem was inspired by a wonderful day, I was privileged to be invited to her majesty the Queen's garden party 2015 in the grounds of Buckingham palace.

Human nature thrives on praise, a thank you given with a smile,
It makes you feel appreciated, loved, happy, life feels worthwhile.
As a simple gesture by the most important lady in our land,
Inviting you to her garden party makes you feel simply grand.
Our noble Queen Elizabeth graciously sends out invitations every year,
To those in our society who have enhanced it with love, inspiration and good cheer.

The Queen appreciates there are those who make this world a happier place,
Helping those in need, the elderly, the sick, inspiring our young folk the future to face.
This world never has enough happiness, contentment, relaxation and cheer,
To those who provide this important ingredient in our lives, we treasure dear.
Look deep into your heart, is there any small act of happiness you can do?
However great or small, it will make you happy and others too.

Our noble Queen sets her examples opening her doors to welcome you all,
To those who give their love, dedication and support to life's ever demanding call.
The Queen's garden parties are a shining light in this troubled world of ours,
It is further enhanced with a display of glorious flowers.
To many who have been blessed to be invited to this event,
It will be remembered as a day of happiness, awe and wonderment.

It is a once in a lifetime invitation for folk like you and me,
Not many get invited to go to Buckingham Palace and join the Queen for tea.
Let us hope the Queen and her heirs will not stop this heart- warming event,
It unites the Royal House with our Nation, praising our good folk, sincerely meant.
On behalf of our visitors I thank you for inviting us here today.
These parties are appreciated; we all hope they will continue to stay.

A copy of this poem was sent to her majesty the Queen, my poem was enhanced and framed; Her Majesty graciously accepted this piece and sent me a letter from the palace thanking me. You can find a copy that you can download and print on my facebook page.
(https://www.facebook.com/people/Terry-Godwin/100009219527909)

Also while you are visiting me via facebook take a look at my other downloadable works the Twin Towers & A Memorable Evening. This particular poem was inspired while I was walking along the Brighton seafront, this poem will be included in my new book We Love Brighton & Hove, coming soon.

21 Pussey's Prospects

Holly the cat lay snug in front of the roaring fire,
She had been brushed, fed and cosseted to her desire.
In the morning in the garden she had caught two mice,
For a day's work she thought that would be suffice.
Coming in from the garden she always sidled against her mistress's leg,
This caressing manoeuvre ensured for nothing she would have to beg.
Holly knew she was spoilt and pampered too,
She was determined to enjoy this indulgence through and through.
Holly reflected and thought she would never give this would a miss,
If she was going to get another eight lives like this!

22 The Dating Game – Part 1

Peter

Peter, sprightly, slightly balding, had a manly figure,
Did he daily exercises, only half an hour but always with vigour.
He was now forty, both his parents had died,
He remembered them with love and pride.
They left him a house and a small amount of cash,
He was a qualified accountant, a steady type, not much dash.
He had two love affairs, both ran about six months apiece.
There were no recriminations when all parties love did cease.

Both his previous loves had their own career,
Didn't want to settle and become a loving and permanent dear.
At forty, Peter was beginning to feel he wanted to be a dad.
To come home in the evening when wife and family to see him were glad.
His two previous loves he had met by chance,
He never regretted either, his life they did enhance.
Now he wanted to meet and love a woman who wanted to become his wife.
Make his house a home and enjoy a family for life.

He was determined to seek out and search further afield,
His limited exposure to his local ladies nothing did yield.
Determined, he now decided to join the dating game,
He set out what he thought he wanted in a woman.
Instructed the dating agency to find the lady of his dreams if they can.
Two of his colleagues had been down this path,
One had taken it seriously, the other for sex and a laugh.

He counselled the first who had been on the dating list for a year,
It took him a while to overcome his nervousness and fear.
But now he felt he had made contact with someone who was becoming most
dear,
He told Peter about his mistakes, always think of your contact.
When you find one you could love give her your fullest attention, charm
and tact.
You are making the biggest decision ever when marrying and taking a wife,
It can bring you great happiness or hell for the rest of your life.

Peter went down to the agency, filled out a deep and complex form,
So much detail he realised this was the norm.
He provided photos of himself smiling and looking happy,
In nature he was gentle and tolerant, this was what he wanted the fair sex
to see.

The charming lady at the agency said she would contact him in a week,
With a selection of ladies who a man like him did seek.
Then appointments would be made to discuss first by phone,
Then you can arrange to meet if you both feel good vibes are sown.

If not, we will find another lady for you to date,
Sooner or later you will find one you will want to mate.
Take your time, take care, but keep the flow moving gently along,
Make sure she sees in your heart a warmth becoming strong,
Peter went home and wondered what the future would hold
Whatever the outcome the future would soon unfold.

The Dating Game – Part 2

Mary
Mary was pretty, good figure, nearly thirty- four.
She was still hoping love would come knocking at her door.
She had boyfriends when she was a teenager and young,
She pretended to love them, then only for fun.
She felt as she could get plenty of admirers then,
It was only a question of saying "Yes" and when.
But it did not turn out that way at all,
She was beginning to feel she had missed out after the ball.

She fell in love and shared her mate's flat,
Then she cleared out, moved abroad, and that was that.
She invited a girlfriend in to share the rent,
Then she got married and Mary was left without a gent.
Mary felt time was passing her by,
To find a lover she must try.
About joining a dating agency she had often thought,
Heard good and bad stories, she didn't want to be caught.

Then she read an article in the newspaper which advised you,
What to expect and what to do.
Yes she decided to sign up, but with who?
Having no experience, she hadn't a clue.
She went on the website and obtained a list,
She felt this was her opportunity not to be missed.
Mary studied lots of agencies literature and their cost,
She preferred a small local one, hoping in it she would not get lost.

Getting involved in a lot of dates, having to sort them out,
Having to say "No" could cause embarrassment no doubt.
She wondered if she would ever be swept off her feet.
After receiving six phone calls she made two dates.
After they had met, had a drink, she said "Goodbye" at the garden gate.
She was slowly getting the rhythm of finding a mate,
She was getting keen and interested in booking an interested date.

The Dating Game – Part 3

Peter and Mary Meet

At the same dating agency where both Peter and Mary had signed on,
Neither knew whether to find their new love would be short or long.
Both were keen to find a love of their choice,
To walk with each other, love and sing with one voice.
Both were invited by the agency to a party for them.
Ten would be ladies and ten would be men.
After being introduced they were left together in a room of their own,
With soft music in the background and an attractive buffet, together they
had been thrown.

To Peter this was not what he had expected,
He intended to be reticent, his social skills not perfected.
He was learning quickly how to be outgoing,
He knew to the ladies his interest in them must be showing.
He approached Mary who had a drink in her hand,
She looked feminine, happy, beguiling as a woman can.
He felt that as soon as he spoke to her,
She responded as her feelings told him were.

Both reciprocated as they both felt an attraction.
Both were cautious at this instant reaction.
Within a few minutes thy were both chatting away,
They found much in common, each had plenty to say.
When the organiser came in to wind the meeting down,
Peter and Mary had arranged to meet for dinner in town.
Mary went home, she was dancing on air,
She felt strongly for Peter, to think of disappointment she did not dare.

Peter went home excited as can be,
He felt he had found a partner who would make him happy.
Three days later they met for dinner.
When Peter took Mary home he felt he had a winner.
Mary too had joy in her heart,
She was sorry that night they had to part.
For two months they met three times a week,
Loving each other's company which they did seek.

Then Mary asked Peter if he would like to stay the night.
Peter accepted the offer with total delight.
A week later Mary received a bunch of flowers with a note,
Would she like to join Peter for a cruise on a friend's boat.
She gladly accepted, she wanted to be with him, he was becoming her man.
Peter on this cruise wanted to spoil her as much as he can.
Then to propose was his lover's plan.

For four days they sailed the sea,
Away from it all they were happy and free.
On the third day Peter produced an engagement ring,
She accepted and Peter's heart did sing.
Two months later they were to marry,
Over the threshold of his home Peter did Mary carry.
This is a story where love won through,
If you too go on the dating game, take care whatever you do.

Ten years later Peter and Mary were sitting around the swimming pool,
Their two boys frolicking, splashing, swimming, keeping cool.
Mary said to Peter, if our boys have any claim to fame,
It is because we met and loved through the dating game.

23 Our Trees

We live in urban Rainham, in the garden of Kent,
We have a garden where trees are in their element.
Our garden is about thirty paces long,
Say it is fifteen paces wide, I can't be far wrong.
The tallest, the oldest at the end of the garden is the wild cherry,
When you see the cherry stones in our lawn, it is obvious the birds have
been making merry.

We have two lilac trees that blossom together,
One blossoms pink, one mauve, a cheering sight in dull weather.
We have two hawthorn trees that demand their space,
Every year a rich supply of berries for the birds table they grace.
We have a very old apple tree,
When it next has a poor crop that will be the end of he.

At the end of the garden next to the wild cherry,
Is an attractive copper beech, producing no fruit or berry.
Its colourful leaves for most of the year are a delight,
Without it our garden would not be such an attractive sight.
We come next to our fruitful plum tree,
We once thought it was a damson, how wrong could we be.

When picked, they make a welcome addition for our tea,
When cooked and preserved with apple they are delicious for me.
At last we come to a tree, obviously a fir and ever green,
It stands like a Christmas tree demanding to be seen.
Everywhere possible the ivy climbs up all the trees bark,
Cutting it off continuously is no lark.

Our trees attract so many birds and house their nests,
We love the birds, a reason to think our trees are the best.
The trees give us shade on a hot summer's day,
Ideal for our grandchildren to sit under and play.
The birds and the trees give us pleasure every day,
We are making sure our trees keep healthy and are here to stay.

24 The Twin Towers Disaster or A True Friend

The Twin Towers in New York was attacked on September 11th 2001 by
terrorist's planes which were crashed into them, killing 2977. On going
through poems sent to me for reading as presenter in the Sunlight Centre in
Gillingham, Kent. England a few years ago, I received this hand written poem,
I cannot find the poet's name who wrote this I think the content is great, so I
have passed it on to you to contemplate. It had no title. I have tidied it up
and added verse to give it a strong finish. It reminds us all that terrorism at
the moment seems far away, but they can strike anywhere and at any time.
Now follows the manuscript as received.

Just an ordinary day on the forty second floor
Till came the explosive crashing sound.
When fire and smoke shot through the lift door
Our tower was a tremor from the roof to the ground.
"Evacuate" came the frightened cry,
"Go quickly down the stairs,
In orderly fashion, we are quite high,
Help each other, stay in pairs!"
Orderly it was, until the thunderous rumble,
Alien sounding screeching as joists began to buckle,
When the walls began to crack and crumble,
We all knew the tower would tumble.

The heat was blistering, masonry falling,
Acrid smoke choking us, people crying, calling,
Mobiles were a Godsend, for fearing we might die,
We had that chance to make our call, perhaps our last goodbye.
In my heart I feared I wouldn't make it,
My tears were falling, I couldn't fake it,
At the best of times my pace was slow,
And the stairs were a route I didn't know.
It would take thirty minutes or more,
To get down to the bottom floor
People were panicking, running for their lives,

Others jumped from windows, taking fatal dives.
 The stairs were breaking up as people rushed by,
Who could blame them, they didn't want to die,
Soon I was alone, stumbling and choking in the smog,
I felt there was no hope for a blind man and his dog.
"Bob", my loyal guide dog,
Was, as always by my side,
Trembling, he guided me through the smog,
And over the bodies of people who died.
Bob had always been more than my guide,
He was family and friend.
I didn't want him by my side.
Until the grizzly end

.

I knew then what I had to do,
"Go Bob, leave" I cried,
If he ran now, he could be safe
He must not stay here, till he died.
I loosened the leash, and shouted" Go" again,
He licked my hand, and next to me he stayed,
I thought, "What's up with Bob, he never disobeys,
"If he stays here, he, till I die,
I thought, dismayed.
Four times I tried to make him go,
His life depended on it, but how could he know,
Although in mortal terror that damn dog would not heed,

No matter how I screamed at him, he would not obey and leave.
My heart was heavy with despair, just one thing left to do,
With angry voice I screamed at him "LEAVE, I don't want you!"
I lashed out with a hefty kick, felt my boot strike bone,
I heard him yelp with fear and pain...and then I was alone.
The stairway walls were hot, oxygen becoming depleted,
I picked me way down, stair by stair; I must not be defeated,
Twisted metal and masonry, walls heaving and shaking,
I even felt the steps beneath my feet disintegrating
Down was the only way to go,
I prayed for my dog, I loved him so,
I hoped that he'd run very fast, and that he'd got free,
I couldn't bear it if he'd died, because he'd stayed with me.

I heard the clattering of feet
Of some fireman coming up
"Keep going, pal, they shouted through the heat
"We saw your dog on the first floor, he's a plucky pup."
"Looks like he has made a dash,
He's limping and he's got a gash.
Someone's trying to calm him down."
I thanked them with a nod and a frown.
I heaved a sigh of great relief,
But what happened next defies belief,
I'd stumbled, then just a I rose,
I didn't believe it, I felt a wet nose.

Touching my hand was a wet doggy.
Whatever my fate was going to be,
My dog, my hero would be with me,
If he was in terror it did not show,
I was the weak one that I know.
With agile body and eyes that could see
He swiftly, surely guided me,
Masonry was flying through the air,
Debris was scattered everywhere.
Down those stairs we fairly flew,
Now sparks and flames shooting everywhere,
We survived somehow, It's true,

We managed to escape with just seconds to spare.
Our wounds were gently tended,
In time, our bodies mended.
But the memories of that fateful day.
Will never ever go away.
Twas just an ordinary day on the forty second floor,
Then it was gone, there are no floors anymore.
Our story's not quite finished; Bob helped me to survive,
My dog, he got a special medal, me .....I am still alive
That night I spent recovering in a hospital bed
A miraculous escape all the papers said.
The reporter's photo'd me till I was black and blue.
I cuddled Bob so the world knew he was a hero too.

That night I don't think I slept at all,
thinking of the crumbling walls and fire ball.
Though I am blind God gave me Bob to compensate
Because of that, I don't stand at heaven's gate.
Two thousand, nine hundred and seventy seven died because of that
terrorist attack,
Tens of thousands will live to endure the terrible flak.
Loss of family, loved ones, colleagues, friends who died,
Will be remembered for many a day.
War is war, and the terrorist who did this terrible deed,
Will meet the "American" revenge soon I pray

With the loss of the twin towers,
America answered the enemy by building freedom tower.
You see why America sits high in the world's freedom hall.
She did not bow to the enemy,
she faced them, and walked tall.
Well done America the free world needs you;
we really appreciate your support in whatever you do.

25 How To Master A Disaster

Life is so full of ups and downs,
We ride the ups, how do we face the downs.
The downs come with disappointment or loss,
When we become despondent or cross.

When we are down we must control our thought,
Think positive, take heed if counsel is given or sought.
If we have lost a dear one, reflect and with care and deliberate,
You have had a shock, now your feelings you must placate.

Often the loss you will never replace,
You are still alive, now the world you must face.
Time will move you gently to a happier place,
How quickly, it must be you who sets the pace.

Think of those around you who love you,
Become not a burden, but smile and help them too.
Always think of the good times you enjoyed with loved ones in the past,
Those memories will remain with you till the last.

If it is your ambition or aim in life that you have lost out,
Stay calm, assemble your thoughts, think positive, that is what it is about.
I always think if you are in good health with a clear mind,
You can look elsewhere, do something else even if it is a bind.

As you sit there and bemoan your fate,
Think of the millions, disabled, desperately poor, grateful to be in your state.
You must think positive, think of your assets you have got,
Think of those who will love you and help you whatever your lot.

Think of the famous men who at first failed, perhaps again and again,
They got up and fought until they unshackled the loser's chain.
A positive and determined attitude is the key to it all,
It raises our spirits to overcome the disasters we befall.

For some of us we have tremendous will to win,
We believe to lose is a disaster or sin.
Maybe the referee or judge had bad eyesight,
That was why the decision against you was not right.

In all life as in sport, skill and determination will win the day,
We all hope and pray that Lady Luck will play her card our way.
You must have the will to win, but accept loss with grace,
To take part in the game is the object, to lose is no disgrace.

Inevitably to revive our spirits whether it be sadness, or on the losing side,
Think positive, think of others, look forward if you want happiness to be
your bride.
What has happened is now in the past, tomorrow is a new day,
Help yourself, others will help too, whether you become happy or sad,
you have the final say.
When it comes to competing the old and tested adage is true,
If at first you do not succeed, "Try, try, try again" and you will win through.

26 Love, Life And Happiness

Where there is pain I wish you peace, mercy and rest,
When you suffer self- doubt I wish you confidence so you can give your best.
Where there is tiredness, weariness, I wish you patience, renewed strength
and understanding.
Where there is fear I wish you love, courage, and to be brave and
upstanding.
When you are trying, I wish you determination, a strong heart to keep you
going.
When you want love I wish you happiness and care to keep the world
flowing.
When you want revenge, to hurt and hate, I cannot condone.
When you praise, love and care for others you will never be alone.
When you want happiness, the joy of living, think positive because that will
be up to you.
Whatever you give the world, the world will do its best to give back what you
are due.

27 I Am A Woman

I am a woman, I want a man who will love me and woo,
I want a man whom I can love too.
I want a man, who will be a loving dad,
Who will teach our children the good from the bad?

I want a partner who will be my partner for life,
I want a man to whom I will be a happy wife.
I want a man who will be my lover, partner and friend too,
I want a man who to me and the family will be forever true.

I am a woman, unashamed that I want a man,
My genes are such I want to make love and mate when I can.
I am a woman, I need a mans seed,
Without him to have a family I cannot succeed.

I am a woman, of a man I need,
Endowed with sex, beauty, femininity and guile,
Mother Nature will help me to succeed.

28 I Hear The Silence

I sit alone on the ocean shore,
Entranced by the rhythm of the tides that I adore.
I feel the wind, its gentle blow,
I hear the silence, it is peace we all love and know.

I sit beneath the stars at night,
The moon bathes me with her magical light.
The passing clouds create shadows of mystical delight.
Night passes, a bright dawn sets the world alight.

The moon, the stars, the wind, the sun are life and soul to me,
Absorbing the silence I feel so complete and free.
The Earth's wonders are great, generous and divine,
We embrace together making my life sublime.

29 I Remember The Lamplighter

The old man sat at his window,
Remembering times of long ago,
His grey hair gave away his age,
His tired body now held him hostage.
Through this window he watched as a boy,
He remembered he was shy, rather coy.
In the evenings he watched the lamplighter go round,
Lighting the lamps, lighting up everywhere around.
He opened the garden gates with care,
To challenge guard dogs he would not dare.
He waved to the children, who waved to him,
Giving a smile and a cheery grin.
At that time chimney pots belched out smoke,
Encouraging thick smog the streets to cloak.
He watched the local bobby, the arm of law,
Treating all with respect, whether rich or poor.
He was our guardian, against the evils of the street,
They kept out of his way when he was on his beat.
I watched with awe as the lamps came to light,
To me the golden lanterns were a comforting sight.
In those days I wanted to be a lamplighter man,
And light the streets as only a lamplighter can.
I was sent away to boarding school.
Where pen and ink became my tool.
To tramp the streets, wet, damp and cold,
Getting dog bites, and many other discomforts I was told,
The romance of being a lamplighter gradually passed away,
I still have a soft spot for the lamplighters whose job was to keep the dark of
night away.

30 When I Knew I Was In Love

In my day a lady's ambition was to marry,
When your chance came rarely did you tarry.
I was twenty four in good condition I would have said,
Still a virgin, never having shared a man's bed.
Saving myself for my wedding day,
Praying for a lover who would soon carry me away.

Available men around here were few and far between,
My girlfriend Tina and I went looking for love as a team.
I worked as a secretary in the rates dept, of the local council.
Only ladies worked there which to me was not brill.
Tina and I always went to the local dance,
So many ladies, so few men, we rarely got a glance.

It was Sunday afternoon when we were walking around the park,
Two gentlemen approached us which we thought was a lark.
They invited us to the park's cafeteria for an ice cream,
We accepted, that should be harmless that would seem,
Jeff and Ted introduced themselves in a courteous way,
Tina introduced myself Betty, all four of us put on our best display.

Instead of ice cream we had cream tea,
We all got on well together especially Jeff and me.
Tina and I both made dates for the forthcoming week,
Going home together Tina and I could hardly with excitement speak.
It was a long way to go, but we felt this could be our big thrill,
We prayed we would not tumble down the hill like Jack and Jill.

Six months later Jeff and I married in the church,
I liked Jeff very much, married, because I did not want to be left on a perch.
I did not want to become a spinster and live alone,
I wanted a family, security and my own home.
For three years we saved hard to buy our own house,
We had a pleasant life, that I had no grouse.

Jeff loved me, there was no doubt of that,
But on the same wicket I just could not bat.
On our wedding night mum persuaded me to buy an attractive negligee,
To inspire Jeff to start our union with a sexual spree.
I wore it for almost a week,
Not happy then lost in the laundry so to speak.
Then I wore a night dress that I was comfortable in,
Not encouraging romance, sex or any other sin.
When Jeff made love to me, there was nothing in it for me,
I would lay back and think of what I could get for tomorrow's tea.
Jeff would kiss and cuddle me when he tried to woo,
I did not respond as a loving wife should do.

Jeff praised and caressed me when he could,
I gently responded, never enthusiastically as I should.
After three years we bought our abode,
A small cottage just off the main road.
It was then I knew I had become pregnant,
It was then I knew on Jeff I was now dependant.

I wanted his love for me and our baby,
I wanted him to hug me as tight as tight can be.
I wanted to be his woman, he to be my man,
I knew I would love him as much as I can.
I went to the dept. Store and bought saucy underwear,
I bought a night dress, I admit it was skimpy, there was not much of it there.
I would cook his favourite meal tonight and declare,
I was pregnant, that would make us a very happy pair.
That was what happened, when I told Jeff he exploded with joy,
We did not care if it was a girl or a boy.
That night we went to bed and enjoyed our love together,
I knew that I would love Jeff with all my heart forever and ever.

31 Your Destiny

If you have found a smile,
The sweetest you have ever seen,
If you have heard a voice that makes your heart beat,
You wonder why, what does it mean?
If you have felt a touch,
That sets your heart aglow,
If you have met someone,
You desperately want to know,
It must be love setting the pace,
Cajoling you to take a lover on.
Be bold and take Adonis's hand,
Act quickly lest it will soon be gone.
Some say love is blind, perhaps that is what,
Mother Nature intended it to be.
When love is true we only see the good,
And do not see what we do not want to see.
If you believe some things in life,
Are meant to be,
Then you have found true love,
And happiness will be in your future destiny.

32 A Great Decision

We at the Medway town have been struck a heavy blow,
We are to lose one of our dignitaries, that is regretfully so.
We have been informed by the press, by wireless and television,
We are to lose a great man of statue and vision.

The Bishop of Rochester Dr. Michael Nazir Ali has made a decision of import,
He feels passionately his energies elsewhere are sought.
He wishes to devote his time in helping the persecuted Christians in Pakistan and Iran,
To give them support, encouragement and make conversions where he can.

The Bishop's opinions and views are listened to with care,
He will voice his thoughts where others should, but do not dare.
He is a great Christian and wants the entire world to be Christians too,
He would like to coerce and wants the entire world to be Christians too,
He would like to coerce the non believers to see his point of view.

He is prepared to give up high office, its privileges and grace,
To go into the wilderness and meet non Christians face to face.
With his determination, charisma, courage and charm,
He wants everyone to enjoy the care of being in the cradle of God's loving arms.

In his high office as Bishop he has received many a death threat,
Because others don't like uncomfortable truths which upset.
He greets you with a smile and enchants you with his quiet persuasive way,
You regret when he has left you, you then realise you wanted him to stay.

Whatever your persuasion, you know a man like this is hard to find,
Who makes such a personal sacrifice to win over the unbelievers of Mankind.
The world is an ever changing place, for good or bad,
The loss of our dear Bishop will make many others needing his comfort glad.

Dear Michael, Bishop of Rochester with full hearts we wish you well,
And pray the Good Lord will be with you and help to bring much happiness to those who come under your spell.

Presented to
The Rev'd Dr Michael Nazir- Ali Bishop of Rochester
By Terry Godwin – The Laughing Poet
On the occasion of
The Gillingham and Rainham Conservatives farewell dinner
On behalf of his many admirers and supporters in the Medway Towns.
We all wish you every success in your future endeavours.

33 Golden Thoughts

A golden thought comes to everyone's mind,
When one is generous and one is kind.

A golden thought when bathed in sympathy,
Wishing to help and comfort those in misery.

A golden thought is when one makes a sacrifice,
When one helps others and pays a heavy price.

A golden thought is created when you see,
The best in everyone and enjoy their company.

A golden thought is there when you hold another's hand,
Giving love and care, showing you understand.

A golden thought comes when you sleep at night,
Determined tomorrow you will do good and put matters right.

A golden thought is when you come last in a race,
And you cheerfully congratulate the winner with a firm embrace.

A golden thought is when you let your loved ones know,
You love them dearly and keep telling them so.

A golden thought is when you see your enemy lies down to die,
You forgive him, bless him, kneel and pray and sadly cry.

Of golden thoughts in this world there is never enough,
That is why so many suffer, find the world cruel and the going tough.
Mankind is born with golden thoughts, if only we would let them flow,
Then brutality, unfairness, wickedness would vanish.
And the world's heart with happiness would glow.

34 A Maiden's Prayer or That Magical Glance

Most young ladies spend a lot of time and effort in making themselves
attractive to the opposite sex. They endeavour to be beautiful at all times,
praying when Mr. Right sees her he will fall head over heels in love with her.
She dreams of a magical glance that will capture his heart.

This poem tells you how Tony and June came together.

I am in love with a wonderful boy,
I am walking on air, full of joy.
I met Tony last week at a dance,
I lost my heart on a single glance.

He asked me to partner him in a quickstep,
I was thrilled, at dancing he was adept.
He asked my name, I told him June,
His was Tony, was he to be my love and fortune?

When we finished dancing he said "Let us have a drink."
My heart was in a whirl, I could not think.
The whole evening he devoted to me,
I asked myself is this how true love should be?
May it never stop would be my womanly plea.

After the last dance he asked if we could meet once more,
He suggested next week on this very dance floor.
As we parted on my cheek he placed a gentle kiss,
This completed for me an evening of bliss.

In bed that night my happiness turned to doubt,
All he knew he was Tony, nothing else I had found out.
Neither of us had taken each other's address,
How stupid of me I did confess.

Well all I could do was to pray,
That we would meet again on the promised day.
That week I tried to cool my ardour,
As each day passed it became herder.

At last the day of the date came,
No other day of my life would be the same.
On that night of the dance I did not know what to wear,
I dressed as feminine as I could taking special care.

I wanted to arrive at the dance fifteen minutes late,
I was nervous as hell I can state.
When I got to the dance hall he was waiting at the entrance,
Waiting for me for his evening entrance.

He paid for my entrance fee, we went in hand in hand,
We danced all night it was simply grand.
We left early so we could have a meal together,
We were forming a relationship we did not wish to sever.

We have been married for over thirty years,
We have had so much joy, not many tears.
I will always remember first meeting the love of my life,
That magical glance until Tony and me to become a happy husband and wife.

35 Farewell Common Sense

Today we mourn the passing of a dear friend,
It is so sad to think common sense has reached its end.
Common sense has been with mankind since the beginning.
Guided humanity with simple answers and a clear seeing.

He was being ousted to death by the regulators of the E.E.C.
Our own parliamentarians joined in with their stupid bureaucracy.
Common sense teaches us to take one step at a time,
Work hard, keep healthy, love and respect each other and all will be fine.

Common sense it was to keep us on the narrow and straight,
Share your problems with your neighbours, sit down and debate.
Our society is now strangled with debt by overzealous regulation,
We are penalised for the smallest error from authority without hesitation.

The poor cannot afford to appeal against the Court's unfair decision,
Without expensive Solicitors your appeal is treated with derision.
A man must not defend with fervour his house any more,
Against burglars or thieves or against the law.

Young children aged six kissing each other are charged with sexual
harassment,
Yet rude young ladies can display themselves without embarrassment.
One is encouraged to borrow more than one can afford,
When you are pushed into bankruptcy the banks will get paid you can be
assured.

You can be fined for putting your rubbish bins out the wrong day,
More bureaucracy is created all the time to make you pay, pay, pay.
School teachers no longer are allowed control of their class,
Exams are now so easy, one must be stupid if they do not pass.

A disabled driver in his car displayed his badge upside down,
He was fined heavily, for him so discretion or mercy was found.
A young thief robs and vandalises the local sweet shop,
When caught his wrist is slapped and told his bad behaviour must stop.

Is it common sense or right that criminals get better treatment than their victims?
Judges dole out sentences according to their moods or whims.
Murder was much lower when sentences were life for a life.
Now we have the culture of carefree youths gladly killing with a knife.

Parents are not allowed their naughty children to smack,
Without a firm parental hand children go off on the wrong track.
Common sense or reason are no longer the order of the day
Disrespect for all, physical violence, drunkenness and drug taking now hold sway.

Young girls, younger and younger join the mothering queue,
In spite of being told what precautions to take and what not to do.
Solicitors ignore common sense, simple indiscretion is kept out of sight,
They want Court cases, which they think is their right.

Innocent victims are given a taste of the Law's bitter bite,
So the Solicitor's bank statement will present a prosperous sight.
Common sense tells the smokers to stop, give it up,
It claims early deaths and a painful life on top.

Common sense, care, love, reason, "How can we persuade you to stay?"
Surely there is hope, can we encourage her, her part to play.
Education of high morals, love and respect must be the way.
To save our dying world, stop all wars, and let peace and happiness rule the day.

36 Goodbye Dad, Goodbye

I stand at my father' grave,
Inside my heart does quietly cry.
I stand at my father's grave,
I knew it was time for him to die.

For the last year he had been in terrible pain,
The surgeon's knife, the healing pill relieved so little.
He wanted to join death so in peace he could sleep again,
For the last six months he agonised in hospital.

Mother had died six years ago, a bitter blow,
Her sudden death was a shock to us all.
To our family she was wonderful, our hero,
Dad took it well, gritted his teeth, walked tall.

Mum and Dad had always been so great together,
To us their three sons we owed them a great deal.
They gave us support whatever the weather,
They gave us encouragement, gave us zest and zeal.

We all knew Dad's death had to come,
When it did we were not prepared.
For Dad it was welcome relief, he was going to join Mum.
From further agony he was going to be spared.

I stand at my Father's grave and cry,
To bid him farewell, my final goodbye.
I feel his relief, his spirit flying high in the sky,
It was God's gift that our beloved Dad should die.

37 The Power Of Happiness

When your spirit is high and you are happy too,
Your happiness is infections, the world will respond to you.
Folks who are sad will appreciate your smile,
Your encouragement will help them over a difficult style.

Happiness will bring our confidence in you,
You will finish tasks, some long overdue.
Happiness and confidence will renew your zest,
Enabling you to give of your very best.

Happiness and contentment and love we all desire,
Not misery, hatred, loneliness and wars of hell fire.
Happiness in man is a state of mind,
In this mood he can be generous and kind.

If only we could invent a happiness pill,
So men to each other would proffer no ill.
What a wonderful and friendly world this would be,
We would enjoy love, care and happiness for eternity.

38 Be Mine, Be Mine

I look into your eyes, admire your smiling face.
I hold your hand and our hearts embrace.
I cannot imagine a future without you,
My love to you will be forever true.

Be mine, be mine, be mine I pray,
Say "Yes" and make it my happiest day.
I cannot wait till you are in my arms as my wife,
For us I know it will be the beginning of a wonderful life.

I know I shall be walking on air all the day long,
My heart, my happiness, my future in your hands belong.
Be mine, be mine, be mine I pray,
Say "Yes" and make it my happiest day.

39 English Ritual

The Indian chief sat in his wigwam,
Telling his tribe of his trip to England.
The Englanders have ritual I will tell you about.
They cut the grass, roll it, so the land is level throughout.

They put up big white sheets on the fields edge,
Not understand, there is already a big hedge.
They bang in three sticks, then another three twenty two yards apart,
Must be very big magic is all I can impart.

Thirteen men stroll out all dressed in white,
In the sunshine they look smart and bright.
A bell rings, two more men walk out into the middle,
With leg pads, flat sticks, why to me that is a riddle.

Then a man throws a ball at a man with a flat stick,
He waves his stick and there is a loud click.
All the men in white give a loud shout,
"Howzat, howzat" and the man with the flat stick walks out.

This ritual is nearly always a great success,
Because the "Mighty One" up there immediately sends down rain in excess.
This ritual is called cricket, it keeps the country side green,
Proof they say because in England no deserts are seen.

40 The Silence of Peace

It was the silence of Peace, it was the silence of Peace.
When the deadly fire of guns did cease.
It was the silence that brought the world mental relief
The Nations had stopped warring, Peace was now their brief.

It was the silence that made us all reflect,
The joy, the caring, and the loving we had all come to neglect.
It was the silence that made us look for a bright blue sky
Knowing there would be a tomorrow and no more had to die.

It was the silence, war ceasing, when we could think of home
When we could touch our loved ones, never again to be alone.
It was the silence, remembering because of war those who now sleep
For so many of our lost ones we now have time to weep

It was the silence when the battle weary learnt to smile again
When the nation's warriors to inflict death no longer had to train
It was the silence when we knew tomorrow's partner would not be death
When families of their fathers would not bereft.

It was the silence – it would give us time to tend the wounded and the
dying.
To repair broken lives we must keep trying, trying, trying.
Dear Peace, Dear Peace you have come at long last
In our hour of need help us lift the World's miseries that wars always
cast.

Since the world began men, tribes, nations, have always been at war
It is mankind's intolerance, greed, bigotry that rules, not peaceful jaw-
Jaw.
The silence has come, dear Lord, help us to keep it that way
Ensure Peace has forever more come to stay.

41 A Summer Sky

The glorious sun was sinking in the west,
The beautiful sky displaying a plethora of colours at their best.
A gentle and warm breeze caressed and warmed our earth,
The evening was glowing creating a memory of great worth.

Stealthily the night and darkness was slowly creeping in,
To lose such a scenic sky seemed a sin.
Night must come so that the world can rest,
So that it can begin a new day with zest.

The night has its own beauty too,
On clear nights there is a galaxy of stars to view.
The full moon beaming down dressed in white,
In the dark her brilliance is a delight.

With the dawn and the rising of the sun,
The world stirs and now a new day has begun.
When summer visits our England,
She is received with joy,
When autumn sidles in, her harvests we enjoy.

When winter arrives the world must rest and sleep,
So our appointment with spring we can keep.
When spring holds its hand the world becomes alive again,
Earth is exuberant and sings with a happy refrain.

42 Is There A Heaven?

(Asks an inquisitive teenager)

If I go to heaven will there be any room for me?
I am told it is a wonderful place to be.
When you die your soul will transport you there,
Everything around you will be delightful and most fair.
I ask myself whether I am good enough to go,
If there is one God, have I had a good life, how will he know?

Around the world thousands are dying every day,
Has he got time to see everyone gets a fair hear say.
When you get there, whatever age you are, do you remain in the state.
Will still born, young children mature into adults and debate?
Will the elderly, the infirm, disabled all of whom have passed their sell by date,
Have their bodies and minds refurbished, that would be great.

Will all the millions in heaven have a universal language enabling everyone to communicate?
Will the religious of the world unite and religious differences dissipate.
How will the culture of the Stone Age man blend in with the teenager of today?
This is all above my comprehension is all I can say.
Will my departed loved ones be up there waiting for me?
That is those in heaven I hope have been good as me.

While waiting how long they be amused, rested, maybe fed,
You go to heaven to be happy, not to become dead.
When in heaven how long will you be there? What will you do?
Will you be there forever or slowly fade into the blue?
The question is "What does heaven mean to you, or what do you expect?
Some believe in the bible quote "Heaven is on earth", this makes heaven suspect.

Since man walked tall, he needed the solace of Gods to support him,
As religion developed, so heaven was created to entice their followers to sing their hymn.
Heaven is the reward for living the life demanded by that religion,
In most cases encouraging good and damming sin.
I am soon to leave you with this thought,
Your religion, your belief is what you have either been brought up with or taught.

At the end of my life do I just die and sleep forever regardless,
Or will I go to heaven if I lead a good life and to God I impress.
Will I travel the other road the world knows as hell?
Where I will be forever listening to the doomsday bell.
I pray there will be a heaven when I die to receive me,
How there can be one is still a great puzzlement to me.

43 A Wonderful Moment

It was a warm summer's night, I remember it clear.
I nestled in the arms of my love most dear.
The air was still, a glorious sunset hung in the sky,
We wanted to hold this moment, not let it pass by.

We rested on the seashore, listening to the waves roll in,
We are in bliss, we don't want another day to begin.
Our eyes meet, telling each other of our love most true,
The compelling message 'I love you.'

We lay on the beach to be enveloped in harmonious sleep,
To dream dreams that our memories will forever keep.
It was a warm summer's night, I remember it well,
When I recall it my heart does swell.

It comforts me now my love has passed away,
And helps me through another long enduring day.

44 Sky High Generosity

I put my case into the luggage compartment and sat down in my assigned seat,
It was to be a long flight from Gatwick before my friends and I again meet.
I had brought a good book and a crossword to keep me company,
With these and two hours' sleep I hope I have a pleasant journey.
Just before take-off, ten British army youngsters come on board,
They sat all around me, I felt honoured and like a lord.

I asked the young man next to me "What is your destination?"
He replied "Cyprus, finish our training for immediate war operation.
After two weeks we shall move on to Afghanistan, straight into front line,
That's we volunteered for, the sooner the better, for us that will do fine.
When we had been in the air for an hour an announcement on the speakers was made.
"From the trolley coming round a hot lunch is available for which five pounds must be paid."

As I reached for my wallet I heard one soldier to another say,
"Didn't expect that, haven't got any money, just have to go hungry today."
I saw none of the youngsters were buying a lunch, could not afford it.
I got up, strolled to the back of the plane where the attendant did sit,
Gave her a fifty pound note and said "Give the soldiers a lunch on me,
I am sure you can rustle up without further charge a cup of tea."

The attendant took my arm with a tear in her eye and said,
"God bless you, in a month's time all these young men could be dead."
After they had been served the surprised soldiers were as happy as can be.
The cabin staff brought me my lunch, a glass of wine, both free.
When finished I headed for the toilet at the back,
A gentleman waiting in the queue said "Great gesture, I want to support you on that track."

He pressed twenty five pounds into my hand, I muttered "Thanks" with a big smile,
"All we are doing is giving a lunch to our heroes if you think for a while."
The planes captain came down the aisle and singled me out.
He said "Please stand up and I will tell you what this is about.
I was an army pilot just on six years ago,
When two old ladies bought me a lunch and said they were proud to do so.

I felt so happy that someone appreciated the important part in life I played,
Risking my life, day in, day out, so many country folk could be saved.
In response to your generous thought and kindly deed,
The cabin staff made a collection from staff and passengers, we sure did succeed,
We collected two hundred and forty pounds which we were all agreed,
We should pass it over to you.
You are a man we trust and will know what to do."

A big cheer went up, I was embarrassed, none of this I did expect.
Two hours later we landed, the soldier's banded together for their next flight to connect.
I went up to their leader, waiting to board the plane to Cyprus,
I said "Your band or warriors now have a bonus   ,
We have collected two hundred and forty pounds to comfort you all on your way.
On behalf of everyone here, in Great Britain too, God bless and have a great day."

When we saw their plane lift off and fly into the sky,
I prayed to the lord he would not let our young men die.
They were on a course that would demand their life,
When fate could direct one or all to take death as his wife.
What we did, we showed our respect, and gave our men a meal or two,
Whenever we can in any way support, we should always be willing to help, and gladly do.

We should honour, respect and praise our service personal when to war They have to go,
Until you have been in the front line of battle, their fears you will never know.

Why should they give their all when they feel we don't care,
Let them know we value them and for them we shall always be there.
Without our soldiers we could all be under the enemy's vicious knife,
If allowed to live it could be a frightening and pointless life.

45 Her Great Day

She entered the church and sat on the nearest pew,
Paid the reverences she thought was due,
The church was cool and quiet in the fading twilight,
The stained glass windows welcomed in the last of the daylight.

Her attention was caught by the instant church bell,
Its harmonious chimes made her heart swell.
In a week's time she was going to be married to a wonderful man,
She would make him happy was her plan.

She had come here to imagine this happy event,
So she could go home relaxed and content.
The wedding day was going to be the greatest day in her life,
At twenty eight she wanted to settle down and become a wife.

She wanted a family, a boy and a girl,
She was so happy her head was in a whirl.
After an hour of prayer and quiet meditation,
She went home to join the family in planning the wedding celebration.

She took the long walk home through the park,
Arriving home when it was nearly dark.
Mum and Dad were at home happy and content,
Preparing with excitement for their daughter's big event.

This was the way that the normal women should take was their view,
So that the family line would continue.
Every day in every nation this scenario is played through,
So that the future of humanity would ensue.

46 I made a mistake

I had made a mistake, I was sure I was right,
To admit it, say sorry, I was wrong, I wasn't that bright.
It was my pride that would not allow me to admit I was wrong,
To admit I had erred to me showed weakness, I wanted to appear strong.

It was clever, not silly so I thought,
To admit a mistake I was not going to be taught.
When the correct answer came to light,
I was so far out, I looked a sorry sight.

It was then my granddad sat down beside me,
Said "You are upset, why I cannot see
So you were wrong, your pride is hurt,
It is only you that thinks you are a jerk."

In this life many times we have to make a calculated guess,
It could be wrong or a complete success...
Everyone who can think one day will guess wrong,
Admit it quietly, say sorry, what's next? Then move along.

A mistake is as important as you make it,
Whatever you do don't have a fit.
Put it behind you and look ahead,
Think of all the good things you have done instead.

In the future instead of being adamant in saying "Yes" or "No",
Why not suggest "I feel this could be possibly so",
That way covers you whether you are wrong or right,
Stops you worrying throughout the day and night.

So many little things we argue and debate,
Often they are unimportant, why not concede, save heartache.
When I was your age I was lucky you see,
My dad told me what I am telling you, makes sense don't you agree?

47 Maria Got What She Wanted

Since she was sweet sixteen Maria always had a strong sexual appetite,
Making love with Mr. Right always gave her delight.
She wasn't sex mad, always took great care,
Which lover she took whenever she started an affair.
She married at twenty one, was determined to be a good and true wife,
Had two children, the joy of her life.

Her husband George always satisfied her passion,
For twenty years their sexual interest was never out of fashion.
Then George fell in love with a woman aged twenty four,
Six months later they divorced, she didn't see him anymore.
Her son and daughter had moved out and away,
Leading their own lives, having their own say.

Maria always wanting to keep George happy desiring her in bed,
Kept herself attractive, could always turn a man's head.
She took a job working at home on a computer,
To make her plan work she needed to be a freebooter.
In her married life she had always been loyal and true,
However hard here sexual urges called to find another love who,
Would satisfy her passionate needs because George was getting tired,
Neither was getting what each other desired.

She was planning to get three men into her net,
To obtain variety, passion and love her heart was set.
She knew what she wanted and she was determined to get,
She wanted one now so that her present passion would be met.
Replies were coming in from her advert in the paper,
She was earnest; she didn't want just a week-end caper.

Maria arranged to meet Tony who was twenty- eight,
She said she was thirty- five, give or take.
They met in a pub with a restaurant beside,
If they fancied each other, then over a meal they could decide.
Tony was quite shy, Maria wondered if he would do,
He opened up as the evening went through.

Maria was warming up, getting very interested,
She felt her efforts here were well invested.
They went back to her place or coffee or what,
On the settee she undid her blouse because she was getting hot.
Tony, who was experienced enough to realise the true situation,
Took her to the bedroom, the right location.

Maria was wearing her very sexy lingerie,
It raised his desire and he began his passionate spree.
An hour later they both lay exhausted and content,
Both were satisfied, all energy spent.
Tony got dressed and kissed her farewell,
Maria knew he would come back soon for another spell.

Tony was the first of her conquests, he came once a week,
Now two more lovers she did seek.
Maria's auntie had died and she had to sort out her estate,
She went to the Solicitors to determine probate.
She met Mr McCullen who was a young thirty-five,
Maria wondered if in her bed she could make him come alive.

Her chances of seducing him were bright,
Ivan picked her up, she was an alluring sight.
They had a great meal and danced the night away,
She danced cheek to cheek, making her femininity pay.
She roused his passion, he wanted her tonight,
She had offered the goodies, now he wanted to bite.

He drove them back to her place and said,
"My love, let me stay tonight and share your bed."
He was strong and full of passion and fire,
They satisfied each other's desire.
Next day was the week-end, they stayed together,
Remaining indoors because of inclement weather.

In the afternoon and evening they were on song again,
That night they slept through, exhausted of passion and pain.
Sunday morning, she insisted he must go,
Her husband would be returning – of course this wasn't so!
She wanted Ivan to realise this liaison was a sexual one,
No serious ties but plenty of discreet fun.

After morning coffee Ivan left, not too down- hearted,
Knowing there was a regular love available and they would not be long parted.
Maria had Wednesday and Friday sorted out to her delight,
Now she needed a lover to fill Monday night.
This took longer than expected,
Many were interested, many were rejected.

Maria wasn't in a hurry but wanted the scene complete,
Then someone answered her advert and made her heart beat.
He was a professor seeking sex and fire,
Someone who could love him and satisfy his desire.
Someone who would not be jealous of his family affections,
Or intrude on his personal life and university connections.

On their first meeting they hit it off together,
To attract him she gave him her best endeavour.
First he talked a lot, then sexually exploded,
She learnt quickly that he was to be gently teased not sexually goaded.
Maria now had her lovers one, two and three,
However long these liaisons would last or fare,
Maria would enjoy today (or night) and she didn't care.

48 I Want To Be Wanted

I want to be wanted, I am a woman,
I want to be caressed and loved by a man.
I have been in love before, it was fine for me,
I was as happy as a woman can be.

They say women were born to take a mate,
Mother nature needs them for a family to create.
I yearn for love, to give my love to,
I want to attract a man who is good and true.

It is not my nature to sit and wait about,
I will dress in my finery and go out.
I will meet my friend, who feels the same as I,
To make two gentleman happy loving us we will try.

They say life is what you make it,
I am good looking, young, eager to make my life a hit,
Tonight we are going to a party at friends full of hope,
To meet young men, free, with whom we would want to elope.

Always keen to stir the passion of our chosen Mr. Right,
We will keep trying till Mr. Right has taken the bite.

49 Just A Thought

Just think before you start to talk, criticise or moan,
Realise other people's feeling are as tender as your own.
Listen with care to other folk's opinion,
Treat them as a friend, not your minion,
Try to understand what they have to say,
And they in turn will support you when you have a grey day.

50 Over The Hills And Far Away

I dreamed I had been out all day,
Over the hills and far away.
Asked what I had seen, I saw the sea,
On the beaches, children splashing about with glee.
I see smiles on every ones faces, that makes me happy,
At home folks are too often sad and snappy.

I see young men and girls dance in the street,
Their exuberance makes this happy picture a treat.
I listen to the buskers playing and strolling along,
Encouraging everyone to join in and sing their song.
I see new lambs frolicking in fields of green,
Peacocks with stunning tails strut with pride and preen.

I hear church bells ring throughout the countryside,
Hear the joy of couples becoming man and bride.
I meet new friends, we dance and play,
I forget my worries and enjoy the day.
In my dreamland there is no bullet or gun,
No one thinks of killing, just enjoy themselves, have fun.

There is no money, so you cannot get into debt,
No gambling, saving a lot of misery, that is a sure bet.
No one is sick, disabled, or ill,
There is no need for a doctor or his pill.
There is no cause to worry, nothing to doubt,
You relax, feel free, if you want, just sing and shout.

Everyone should visit my land, the land of faraway,
Everyone is equal, everyone can have their say.
There is love and comfort where ever you look,
No place for the wicked, or the sly crook.
When you are sad or depressed, join me in my land of far away,
It will uplift your spirit and help you have a great day.

51 Country Ways

The Texas Rancher galloped over to his neighbours spread,
To talk to Tom Jones about his worries, but instead,
When he knocked a boy of nine opened the door.
The rancher said "Could I speak to Tom, it is important I am sure?"

The boy replied "Dad's out, gone to town."
The rancher pressed on "Can I speak to your mum?" he said with a frown.
The boy replied "She is not here, gone with Dad too."
"How about your brother Howard, he would do."

The boy replied "Howard is away for the day,
Can I help in any other way?
I know where the tools are and where the horse tackle is kept,
You can borrow our old ford, but the engine is suspect."

The rancher carried on "I would like to talk to your Dad about your brother,
He had made my daughter pregnant and he is her lover."
The small boy said "I don't know the answer to that one,
But Dad's charges for his stallions are a thousand dollars all said and done."

I will give him your message and he can invoice you,
You can pay cash, by cheque or credit card too."

52 A Fiddler Came To Play

A fiddler to our village came today,
Turned up and merrily began to play.
Doors and windows were flung open wide,
Dancing feet were not to be denied.

The fiddler experienced knew how to make your heart ring,
His lively music would make the world sing.
Our village folk stopped their chores and joined the dance,
On the cobble stone they jigged and pranced.

There were smiles and happiness everywhere,
We forgot our woes, we were without care.
From the beginning the fiddler played with a lively bite,
Played for an hour, gave us all great delight.

He raised our spirits, we all felt happy and bright,
Seeing the villagers' romping and turning was quite a sight.
For an hour our village was cheerful and gay,
Everyone cheered and blessed him when he waved goodbye and went on his
way.

Where he came from we do not know,
His brief visit set all our hearts aglow.
We hope he will come again very soon,
He revived us all, he was such a boon.

53 Don't Criticise

It is so easy to criticise,
To criticise is often so unwise.
You may be justified, or possibly not,
Not happy with what you have got.

Criticise your friends and you will lose them fast,
Praise them and your friendship will last.
The world says "Cry and you cry alone,"
The world has little time for those who moan.

The world says "Laugh and the world laughs with you,"
So smile, praise, laugh whatever you do.
Would you like to care for a moaning grump?
Others would not either, consign you to the rubbish dump.

It is so easy to criticise,
To criticise is often so unwise.
Think of ways to praise, say "God bless you."
Thank everyone for whatever they do for you.

They will be pleased to help you again and again,
Instead of avoiding you to catch their train.
You may be in pain or discomfort, it happens to us all,
Praise those who support, don't make a bad tempered fuss.

You have been hard done by, out of luck,
You feel miserable, now passing the buck.
Think of the millions of people in the hard world out there,
Little food or water, no medical help, in despair.

Think how lucky you are, smile and think positive,
Accept your position and the life you live.
It is so easy to criticise,
To criticise is often so unwise.

This short love story tells us beauty is not everything, Finding a partner who responds to you, cares, shares the same interest, and needs your love as much as you need theirs, these qualities often more important than beauty which can be cosmetic. These qualities are important building blocks for a long and happy partnership.

54 I Thought Love Had Passed Me By

When born as a girl I was not pretty,
I was called a plain Jane, mores the pity.
Our parents loved their three daughters very much,
I was the youngest of this female clutch.
In those days of not so long ago,
A young ladies future depended on marrying and satisfying her husband's desire and ego.
If you remained a spinster life could become very hard indeed,
Difficult for a lady alone in the world to succeed.

All parents taught their daughters with the greatest of care,
How to cook well, always to look pleasant and fair.
How to manage their home, control the children too,
Not to only marry him, but hold onto him you must do.
My two sisters, both pretty married quickly and well,
When I was eighteen it seemed I was not going to hear my wedding bell.
So I decided to train to become a nurse,
It would be a hard life, but other options looked worse.

I left home and moved into hospital accommodation,
That alone was comfortless and full of depravation.
I became a qualified nurse in four years,
To my parents that brought comfort and cheers.
In those four years I had made one good friend,
Without her companionship I would have gone round the bend.
We were both determined to see the bright side of things,
To live a life without the comfort of wedding rings.

One day into my ward came a very sick man,
The doctors thought he now only had a very short life span.
He had a virus, the doctors did not know what,
He was delirious, his temperature was very hot.
He seemed in a trance, hardly moved at all,
Then on the second night his temperature did rapidly fall.
He had stumbled into the hospital, no one knew his name,
There was no one to care for him which seemed a shame.

Whilst in our ward he had never been to sleep,
Until he did, he would weaken, and away his life would seep.
As I adjusted his bed he asked me to hold his hand,
I instantly responded, held it, it was not as I planned.
His weak hand held mine firmly and did not want to let go,
He smiled, closed his eyes and into deep sleep he gently did go.
When he released my hand I felt a wonderful glow,
His touch, his need, made my womanly feelings warmly flow.

The matron who had seen all this happen said to me,
"It seems holding your hand was good for the patient's therapy,
You must do it again if the patient asks you,
If it comforts him to relax and sleep then that you must do."
Our patient slept the whole night through,
Why, the doctors had not a clue.
Next day when I returned to the ward,
He had asked for me all on his own accord.

He wanted me to hold his hand and sit beside him,
Knowing how busy the nurses were I thought his chances were dim.
I don't know if the matron had a fancy for this young man,
When asked said "Yes, he only has a short life left, let us make him as happy as we can."
As we sat and talked for short periods at a time,
I found out he was called Tony and a Solicitor in his prime.

He had no relatives alive, no girl friends at all,
How he ended up in this hospital he could not recall.
When he dozed off, I would leave his bed,
Help the other nurses and get myself fed.
After a fortnight the amazed doctor diagnosed he was recovering,
I felt this too, to me this was a wonderful thing.
I was beginning to love Tony, but did he love me?
My friend warned me that Solicitors don't marry nurses, my heart did agree.

When he recovered, his old self and was free,
Would he remember my touch, my care, remember me?
How I sympathised, encouraged using my female guile,
Bringing him confidence, regaining his smile.
A week later I was ordered back to carry on full nursing care.
Every day we would smile, sneak a quick chat when we dare.
I could feel his eyes looking to see me whenever he could,
My future felt uncertain, was I to be disappointed, or could it be good.

At the end of each shift I would call in and see,
How he was feeling, it was then he kissed me.
He said "Friday I will be fit enough to go home,
Will it be possible to continue our friendship,
I do not like living alone.
My heart jumped, was he hinting that he wanted to marry me.
I said "Yes but as a nurse I do not get much time free.
We are always so busy, we get no concessions."
Tony smiled "Then I must make our courtship as quickly as I can,
To woo you and make me a happy man."

Four weeks later he bought me an engagement ring,
I was walking on air, how my heart did sing.
Two months later we were married in a church near my parent's home.
My mum and Dad were delighted as I was no longer alone.
At our wedding day my sisters came with their families in tow,
Reminding me I too wanted a family to make my heart glow.
I left the nursing service and moved into Tony's house,
I now had my home and was now my husband's spouse.

Later in our marriage Tony said to me,
"I fell in love with a lovely lady who cared and encouraged me,
Nobody has ever done that to me before, I can assure you,
Your gentle touch, kind words, your smile, the like before I never knew.
You wanted a family, a loving man, we make a wonderful pair, don't you agree.
I nodded in agreement and said "Yes my love I do as you can see."
When I was young I thought love had passed me by.
But found someone up there, always close and nearby,
Found me you so my love I can evermore gratify.

55 Did They Touch?

He died upon the battlefield,
At the time his baby son was born.
He wasn't going to see,
The coming of his son's first dawn.

The death of one, the birth of another,
Father and son, never to touch,
The loss of their child by father and mother,
The babe, his father's loving arms never to clutch.

Did father and son pass each other at the doors of life and death?
Did they touch, did their tearful eyes meet,
Before the babe felt the fathers love and caress,
Or did fate cruelly decide they would never touch or greet.

Sally, nearly sixty was a widow,
Losing her husband came as a terrible blow.
He was killed in a car accident five years ago,
When he died, the world she did not want to know.
The insurance company paid out substantial compensation,
Together with Bill's life insurance, she would have no financial worries in her life's duration.
She had no close family to turn to,
Only a bachelor brother who was fifty two.

It took Sally four years to come out of her shell,
Meanwhile she had lost her friends and those who wished her well.
Now she needed love, now she needed companionship,
She wanted a loved one whose hand she could grip.
The she received a letter from her brother, who was ill,
Requesting she visited him helping him out until,
He could cope again and run his own home,
He was depressed, just hated being alone.

He lived down south in the town of Bartholomew,
He lived in a two bed roomed house with a wonderful view.
Regarding house matters or maintenance he had not a clue.
Now he was ill, he didn't know what to do.
He was a professor at a local university,
He had lived a life free of illness and adversity.
He had a few bachelor friends, who could not help him out,
He needed the support of a good woman there was no doubt.

He knew his sister was alone, perhaps with little to do,
In his hour of need could she come to his rescue?
She came quickly, responding to his call of help and need.
When she arrived at his house, he looked very sick indeed.
She insisted he went and stayed in bed until further notice,
While she rang the doctor and took his advice.
He told her the virus was a very nasty one,
How long it would take to recover was the guess of anyone.

He should be kept warm, get plenty of sleep and rest,
How strong he would be put to the test.
Sally surveyed the kitchen, the bathroom, his bedroom, they were a total mess.
Only his den and office were tidy – more or less.
She looked in his refrigerator and larder, both were nearly bare,
She would have to go shopping, especially for a sick man's fare.
She checked up to see if all his medicines were there,
She made a list of his needs to purchase to benefit his welfare.

Sally ordered a taxi and went to the super store to shop,
She felt great, she was caring for someone, and she didn't want this feeling to stop.
When Sally got back after two hours of shopping she was shattered,
She didn't care, it was her patient that mattered.

The kitchen needed cleaning, she did that first,
Then she made him a hot drink to quench his thirst.
It was a week before he started to show an improvement,
He smiled and said "Thank you," that made her content.
In the meantime she set about cleaning and tidying too,
There was such a pile of washing to do.
After a fortnight the patient came downstairs,
He was thrilled at the way Sally had looked after his affairs.

He gave her a huge kiss to show his appreciation,
She instinctively hugged him giving her a warm sensation.
She remembered when she was only ten years old,
Ted was only two, she spoiled and cuddled him, too much she was told.
At twelve Sally was sent to boarding school far away,
For the next six years that was where she was to work and play.
When she came home for the school breaks and holiday,
Ted was growing up and going his own way.

She turned her love to the natural way of life,
She wanted to be beautiful, desirable, become a loving wife.
She married and settled down when she was twenty three,
She was infertile and did not produce a family tree.
Now she was back with her brother, whom she had loved so much,
As a woman she now thrilled to his manly touch.
For the next two weeks they showed their fondness for each other,
Though sister and brother, both felt each was becoming a lover.

It was four weeks since Sally had come to visit Ted,
She was getting worried she was going to be asked to go to bed.
She announced she had to go home, private matters to attend to,
Confident Ted was getting better and that he knew.
He did not want Sally to leave him in his wilderness,
He wanted her to stay and enjoy their company and happiness.
Ted said "Sally, no one here knows you are related to me,
Change your name back to the name you were born with, and you will see.

We could live together as husband and wife,
You would become the joy of my life.
To the outside world we could say we are going away to be wed,
Come back home to share our home and bed."
Sally was taken aback and quietly said,
"Sounds a wonderful idea, let me ponder on it Ted,
I am going home now, I really have matters I must attend do.
In a few weeks time I will give my answers to you"

Next day she packed her bags and went home by train,
Parting for both was such a strain.
Four weeks later Ted received a letter,
As he read it, it got better and better.
It said "Dear Ted, I thought your proposition through,
Now I am sure what I want to do.
I am putting my house on the market, I am coming to live with you.

The name I was born with, I am going back to.
I am reaching out for love, to begin life anew,
As one gets older, chances like this are few.
My love I shall be joining you on Saturday for tea,
Make sure you keep your bed warm for me."

57 The Price Of Freedom

The Queen in a castle in the days of old,
Though a Queen, she had to do what she was told.
She dressed in clothes, regal, heavy, the fashion of the day.
On any important matters, trivial ones too, she had little say.
When court was held she sat beside the King,
She dared not speak out of turn or say anything.
She learnt to smile and thank visitors, everyone,
For their King's support, whatever deed they had done.

Then at one of the King's feasts she saw,
Where there were many jesters, fire eaters and entertainers galore,
A sad looking monkey sitting patiently on his perch,
Waiting to do his tricks, if not he got the birch.
The Queen said to herself, is that monkey the image of me,
To do his tricks at beck and call, never to be free.
She resolved there and then she would seek another life elsewhere,
Escape from the castle, where to, at this moment she did not care.

She knew a band of gypsies would soon be coming her way,
She planned to join them and run far away.
It was arranged she would meet the gypsy's chief,
To discuss her plans and set out her brief.
When they met in secret, she went in her royal dress,
To the gypsy chief this did not impress.
He pointed out her regalia she would have to leave behind,
Daytime dress for gypsy women must be practical, simple, not refined.

"I don't care" she said "I just want to be free,
Travel the countryside and importantly just to be me.
I hate my crown, the state affairs, being told what to do,
That is why I want to escape with you."
The gypsy chief said "Your ladies wait and serve on you all the day,
How will you survive without them, tell me I pray.
You wear fine shoes, smart and neat,
When they wear out you will have to walk in your bare feet.

Each day you toilet in the privacy of your own room,
Once a gypsy, we share everything and see each other groom.
Your ladies provide water to wash in, no doubt warm,
Our streams are cold, sometimes dirty, hope they won't cause you harm.
Our daily bread is coarse, bitter and often dry,
To your sweetbreads, cakes and wine you must say goodbye.
Are you prepared to walk miles and miles in the sun and rain?
Even our most hardy struggle and feel the strain.

Your grave will most probably be a passing ditch,
When you die no one will care because you are not rich.
I realise you want to feel free and roam this good earth,
Not always easy for folk born of royal birth.
Life for the poor is very hard indeed,
You spend your days trying to stay alive, only the strong succeed.
Because of hunger you take a chicken or grain from a farm without paying,
If caught, because you are a gypsy from the gallows you will swing."

The Queen said "Stop, stop, do not go on.
To join you now I see I would be wrong,
My heart breaks, I fear I could not join you,
I would not be free, I could not live as you do.
I feel I must go back and be a Queen to my king,
If I want comfort, security, I must dance like the monkey on his string.
I realise now most of the world is worse off than me,
Roaming the world, living in poverty is not being free."

The Queen got back to her room, her absence unknown,
She would again play her part in supporting the King and throne.
Meanwhile the King ordered the gypsy chief to meet secretly as agreed,
Gave him a small purse of gold as his mission did succeed,
In convincing the Queen to stay with her King,
The king realised he loved the Queen, and he must treat her as a loved one,
Not just as a chattel or obedient thing.
The King wanted loyalty, most importantly he needed love too,
He now must treat the Queen as a woman and respect her point of view.

58 Philosophy!!!

A man with one watch knows what the time is,
A man with two or more could be in a tizz.

Look at the future through your windscreen ahead,
Not at the mirror with yourself in bed.

Don't look where you slipped down and fell,
Avoid for it next time, remember it well.

Be nice to everyone on your way up,
Because when coming down you may have to share their cup.

Never explain, your friends will not need you to,
Your enemies will not believe you, whatever you say or do.

When seeking revenge, dig two graves you are well advised,
One for yourself, one for your enemy, whatever the outcome, neither will be surpised.

Courage is not the lack of fear to wit,
But the ability to act when facing it.

You have to do your own growing, be at your own beck and call,
It doesn't matter if your dad was weak or strong, short or tall.

The best way to predict your future you know,
Is to create it, build it brick by brick, come rain or snow.

59 Enjoy It Today, Be Damned Tomorrow

In the old days our parents told us about the birds and the bees,
In case you don't know what that was, it's about sex if you please.
For unmarried ladies to become pregnant was a disaster indeed.
She paid the price if this advice she did not heed.

There was no single mother support in those days you know,
She would be in deep financial trouble if she had no family support in tow.
Families not so long ago would not support a wanton daughter,
One who had become pregnant before being wed at the altar.

Her lover if he was a cad, would walk away without a care,
To try his luck again with another lady most fair.
He would mate with another having no shame,
Until she was pregnant, leaving her with the blame.

A young girl wishes to become a woman as quickly as she can,
Will want to see how speedily she can entice a man.
She will thoughtlessly give in to satisfy her sexual desire,
She is thrilled because her beauty sets him on fire.

Teenagers of both sexes will profess to know it all,
Advising them of the risk is like talking to a brick wall.
Young folk today drink, smoke, have sex to excess,
Sooner or later it will bring them and their loved ones much distress.

For teenagers the cautious and wise will try to impress,
The danger of drink, smoking and sex, often with little success.
Mother Nature brings puberty earlier and earlier to the female sex,
The irresponsible male enjoys the pleasure and power he is able to flex.

The problem of uncontrolled sex creates many an undesirable birth,
Accompanied with disease which spreads quickly around our earth.
How to prevent this is a problem to us all,
Because our teenagers cannot, will not, resist Mother Nature's call.

Always be upbeat says the policeman on the street.
Make your customers love you and your products advise the wise man.
Keep driving along quips the professional golfer.
Always keep a trick up your sleeve says the magician.
Think big, fly high, advice passed on by the aviator,
Don't let the competitors eat you up mumbles the alligator.
Seek new solutions, new ideas and hints the inventor.
Keep your enthusiasm alight states the fireman.
Always have a spark of daring in you utters the electrician.
Have the occasional fling the Highland Scot chuckles.
Make a sound business foundation on cement not sand the architect quotes.
Cross your bridge one at a time the traveller tells you.
Praise, praise, never criticise, says the priest, sound advice and very true.
Be ever ready to bounce back if you fall the tumbler advises all.
Listen to all advice with care, says the voice of experience out there.
Don't bottle up all your worries the milkman with experience expounds.
Set yourself an attainable goal and win the match advises the footballer.
When walking on thin ice take great care says the wise old polar bear.
Don't let your competitors run rings around you beams the hoop-la boy,
Dedication, hard work and honesty will be the key to your success said the locksmith.
Have back up, don't run out of steam quips the steam engine man.
Don't chicken out when the going gets tough says the doughty farmer.
Try not to hurt others and cause pain says the window cleaner.
Patience can be a good card to have in your hand says the bridge player.
Stick to your principles says the tube of glue.
Don't get the hump when you are deserted hoots the camel.

Whew! Reading all that, so that I can become a success.
I am afraid all that I cannot address.
If I had an ambition to get to the top and become wealthy too,
Then all these suggestions I must consider and do.
I think everyone who has passed their knowledge and experience to me,
I am afraid I shall remain just little old ordinary me. (Sorry.)

61 The Way It Used To Be

She had kissed me; I wanted to fly high,
She had kissed me, with happiness I wanted to cry.
Of course I have been kissed many times before,
But not by the girl I have come to adore.

I met Mary only a few weeks ago,
When I first saw her she set my heart aglow.
When I asked her out to dinner and she accepted,
I was over the moon because I had not been rejected.

Tonight I had walked Mary home from the dance,
We walked arm in arm, I was in a trance.
When we got to her parent's front door,
She kissed me like I have never seen before.

She whispered "Mum and Dad invite you to come to Sunday tea,"
I gladly accepted, I was happy as I could be.
Tonight I lay in bed in tremulous delight,
Thinking this has been such a wonderful night.

62 If I Was God For A Day

If I was God for a day, what would I do?
If I was God for a day, I would have to think it through.
I would cure those sick and ill, in agony or pain,
Make them strong so that they will not become poorly again.

I must create love in all men's hearts so they will not fight,
Install in them justice so they will do all things right.
To make men believe all women and men are equal,
If they don't, devastating wars will always be the sequel.

Many of the world's problems are created by men's greed,
They care not for those they trample on to succeed.
I would place more power with the gentler female,
Who are more in touch with the world, do not their ambitions on others wish
to impale.

Men must be competitive, that is the nature of the game,
They must be strong so that evil they can tame.
In a day to install love, kindness, justice and tolerance,
Into mankind, not even God the Almighty would stand a chance.

63 The Ticking Clock

The clock ticks, time slips unnoticed quietly away,
Minute by minute, hour by hour, day by day.
Use it wisely when you work, love and play.
It moves on relentlessly come what may.

Shall we do it tomorrow or another day?
Some lose time as they let their thoughts stray,
Dithers let time escape and get away,
Man's time on earth is a short span they say.

You must monitor it carefully and make time pay,
Make your time on earth productive and gay.
Father time will win, you cannot hold him at bay,
Use your time carefully and have a great day.

Tick tock, tick tock, time has moved on again I hear you say,
Live with it, work with it, love with it as you may,
Don't let it become your master in any way.
Enjoy every moment of life on earth during your stay.

64 I Am What I Am

I am what I am,
"What is that you ask me,"
Am I genuine or just a sham,
Am I innocent or guilty.

I look in the mirror and what do I see,
I see myself, am I a fool or a clown.
Am I a man of the church or religion free,
Am I a man of the people or wear a crown.

Am I a man well educated, a man of society,
Am I a man who recovers quickly when knocked down,
Am I a man sober, a man of propriety,
Am I a man timid or a cavalier about town.

Am I a man who relishes the chase,
Am I a man who is definite and strong.
Am I a man the ladies love to embrace,
Am I a man who needs to belong.

Am I a man who is ambitious, loves a dare,
Am I a man who loves to entertain.
Am I a man full of compassion and care,
Am I a man with an intelligent brain.

Am I a man who listens and leads from the front,
Am I a man who shuns publicity.
Am I a man who is never wrong, lets others take the brunt,
Am I a man of complexity or simplicity.

Am I a man who is either good or bad,
Am I a man of honour, who will always stand by you.
Am I a man who is single or wants to be a proud dad,
Am I a man who is responsible, or does not care what I do.

You ask me so many questions, I do not have time to reply,
I have an urgent appointment, must not let me client down.
I have a train to catch, now I really must fly,
I will answer your questions tomorrow when I am back in town.

P.S. Tomorrow never comes so I will answer these questions bye and bye,
I am what I am, and always give my best, I really do try. Tell me, who
are you?

65 Wet Feet --- My Treat

The tide was creeping in on the sandy shore,
It was a warm summers evening which I adore.
Sea horses were frolicking and dancing in the sea,
In the gentle breeze I let my hair blow free.

I walk along the beach, I let the ebbing tide bathe my feet.
The sea birds, the gulls, the terns are here to eat,
The worms, the mollusc, small crabs are their treat.
To me this is a joy, I could forever repeat.

The birds squawk and complain when I walk their way,
Forgive me when on their patch I do not stay.
I have an hour before the tide will drive me onto the quay,
An hour of pleasure and delight as I amble on free.

I relax, I meditate, I dream as I walk this heavenly part of nature alone,
I am in a mood with the world to reconcile and atone.
It is not often I catch the tide and weather in this captivating state,
When I do, I bless the sea, the wind, the golden sand and just luxuriate.

66 Who Has Seen The Wind?

Who has seen the wind today, not you or I?
I have felt his caresses as he passes by.
On a hot balmy day he is heaven sent,
On stormy nights, his fury he vents.

He brings in the clouds, the tempest and the storm,
Their destruction makes the world feel forlorn.
When he is a gentle and a caressing breeze,
He scatters the seeds and fruits of trees with ease.

The winds of this earth are a mighty force,
Great ships like match sticks are blown off course.
The wind provides energy and cleans our air,
When it is aroused, don't challenge it, take care.

The wind can make the sea into a frenzied mass,
Or allow our lakes to calmly reflect like a looking glass.
The wind controls the lives of our men at sea,
They all realise they are always at the sea's tender mercy.

The desert sands grow bigger and bigger each year,
The desert wind creates this phenomenon it would appear.
Our landscapes are shaped slowly, sometimes quick,
It topples magnificent trees like breaking a stick.

It moves hot and cold streams of air about,
It is the provider of our good or bad weather there is no doubt.
The power of the winds of the earth touch every living thing,
They can cause havoc, distress, or joy and make our hearts sing.

Who has seen the wind today, not you or I?
I have felt his caresses as he has passed me by.

67 What A Night That Was!

We met at our local dance,
I wanted to have sex if I got the chance.
I met a man, handsome, tall and slim.
Yes I admit I really did fancy him.

When we danced I shamelessly said,
"I do fancy taking you to bed."
Just as shameless he replied,
"Dear lady your wish will not be denied."

We went back to his car,
He said "My flat isn't very far,
Let's enjoy the comfort of a warm bed,
After that from my fridge we can be fed."

I was thrilled, he was a passionate guy,
He stripped me, caressed me, kissed me, "Oh my."
When he finished it was a job well done,
Both of us enjoyed it, so much fun.

We went to the kitchen for some wine and a snack,
We nibbled and sipped, I said "I would like to go back."
He said "Sure thing, but a telephone call I must make,
Go back to bed where we can rattle and shake."

Ten minutes later, to me it seemed an eternity,
As I lay in wait to join the passion fraternity.
I hit the top, it was great to be a woman,
I wondered vaguely "Is this how the world began?"

We laid together for an hour or more,
I said "I don't want to be a bore,
It is very late, can you take me home?
If not a taxi I will have to phone."

He took me back in his car,
The night was dark, I saw both moon and the Northern star.
Neither of us spoke a word the journey through,
We had enjoyed our sex, we would part without ado.

To this day we never made contact again,
I don't believe he ever gave me his real name.
I have no regrets, he gave me what I needed,
We were both satisfied, enjoying our sex we had succeeded.

Anonymous we met, anonymous we parted, all passion spent,
To me that memorable night was heaven sent.

68 Why Do I Cry?

Why do I cry?
Because I feel so alone, that's why.
I am parted from a wonderful guy,
I still adore him, that's no lie,
However hard I try.
Thinking of him brings tears and a sigh,

We had been together three years, that's bye the bye,
Seemed our relationship cemented no permanent tie.
I caught him loving another woman, he had no alibi,
I could not forgive him, however hard I try.
I feel so alone, now you know why,
I feel so crushed,
I want to die.
Please go away I just want to cry.

69 A Piece Of Heaven

There is a place I want to be,
With my truelove next to me.
In my dreams I know it well,
It is a piece of heaven I can tell.

I stand by a river under the osier tree,
I hear the water gurgling by, gently and free.
The sun gleams to make this a glorious summer's day,
A galaxy of beautiful flowers responds to its warming ray.

I look up entranced into a clear blue sky,
Admire a flock of birds flying free and high.
We relax and sit in the trees welcoming shade,
All life's problems and misfortunes disappear and fade.

We hold hands, kiss and walk in the silent bliss,
This is our heaven, there is no other place like this,
The address of this place we do not know,
A place of peace, love, contentment where we wish to go.
Dear Lord, when our time has come, please make it so.

70 A Soldier Returns To Wootton Bassett

I come home to rest,
I gave of my best,
I died for Queen and country,
My friends and family.

Tomorrow was my birthday,
I planned to celebrate it,
Hip, Hip, Hooray.
Fate decide it was not to be,
Instead of partying,
I am in a coffin as you can see.

As the transporter flies me in,
I hear no cheering,
Wootton Bassett stands in silence in the rain,
My loved ones emotions take the strain.

When I left England no one noticed me,
I return in my coffin as a celebrity.
The armed forces of Great Britain owe a great debt,
To the town of Wootton Bassett for paying our dead such homage and
respect.

71 A Time Will Come…

A time will come when you must stand still,
To take stock of your life in order you can fulfil.
Your hopes, your dreams, your aspirations, your destiny.
To go forward or backward the choices can be few or many.

The decisions taken will be important to you,
You may live with them your whole life through.
The decision you take could be tough for your loved ones and friends too,
If you want to go forward then that is what you must do.

You must be determined, think carefully to give of your best,
When decided, your actions you must do with zest.
It is important you think with a positive mind,
Being positive, solutions are easier to accept and find.

You may find it more compatible to let friends and family push you around,
Allowing this you may never progress or get off the ground.
Still the choice is yours when you stand still and deliberate,
Everyone, somehow, somewhere, sometime can help to determine their own
fate.

72 Change

Change, the older we get,
The harder it is to accept.
Our bodies and mind reject.

Change disturbs our comfort zone,
It affects all elderly, you are not alone.
New ways make us accident prone.

Our established ways, wrong or right,
We will fight change with all our might.
They may our comfort zone blight.

Where born we accept matters as they are,
The young learn, mature, a progressive future is their star,
Our body and mind ages, we can only go so far.

Our young rightly fight to overtake us,
They absorb the changes of the world without fuss,
Eventually they will take charge that is obvious.

Change in this world is vital if we are to progress,
The old must bow to the young and encourage their success.
In this world the young will seek new ways to address.

We oldies must accept the worlds changing ways,
Look to the future, not harp back to the "Good Old Days,"
Accept the inevitable, swim with the flow, it pays.

73 An Apple Scrump To Remember

It was the day the National Health Service started,
For me it was a long time from home I was to be parted.
When I was just fifteen to White Oak hospital I was sent,
They specialised in eye problems and were situated in Kent.
It had ten cottages, each housing 12 girls or boys,
To become their home to be cured and enjoy.

Each of us knew we would be there for six months or more,
Hard to accept, but to save your eyes that was the score.
The hospital had a school, a football pitch, a treatment room and a large
orchard too.
The orchard was out of bounds, that everyone knew.
There was a six foot fence built around it with nails stuck in the top,
For scrumpers and vandals it was there to discourage and stop.

I gave you these details so you will understand my plot,
To acquire some of those delicious Cox's Pippins I had to give my best shot.
Most of the patients were very young, at seven o'clock they went to bed,
Derek, the same age as me, was allowed to stay up until eight instead.
It was during this hour that we planned to go on our scrumpage,
We needed tools to climb the fence which we were to engage.

From the school's carpentry class we borrowed pinchers, an important tool,
We acquired an old blanket from the gardener's shed, sitting on his stool.
We had a bag in which our parents brought goodies on visiting day
To hold the apples we collected on our scrumping fray.
In the wood next to the orchard two small logs we found,
We would use them as a ladder to get over the fence – off the ground.

One of the logs we would tip over to the other side,
Our clever plan to scrump apples was not to be denied.
We would be able to clamber back you see,
To be stuck on the other side would spoil our plan – wouldn't you agree?
From the top of the fence with the pinchers we pulled out the nails one by one,
I put the nails in my pocket, and then replaced them when the deed was done.

The blanket we placed on top of the fence to soften our climb over the top,
Didn't want any splinters or anything else that could catch us on the hop.
Just to scrump some apples all this planning must seem over the top.
In those days in hospital for anything interesting to do, there wasn't a lot.
Anything to break the monotony and boredom was seized upon,
To help pass a dull day quickly and see it gone.

We didn't want anybody to know that we had been on this scrump
Or how we did it – we hoped it would stump.
We both decided to bring back an apple for each of the others in our ward,
When we told them about this their spirits soared.
On the big night it was a glorious summer's eve,
This was our opportunity we were not going to leave.

We went to the fence and got over and back it worked like a treat,
We picked beautiful apples which made our joy complete.
As we ambled back to our cottage my apple I did eat,
Derek decided to eat his in bed and savour tonight's feat.
We got back to the cottage and Derek went into his ward,
He gave everyone an apple and felt like a lord.

I went into my ward and gave my apples out,
My five mates were delighted without a doubt.
The night nurse visited each cottage three times a night,
When she tucked in little Johnnie, his apple came into sight.
She asked him how he got it and he said everyone got one too.
She searched all the other beds and caused quite a to-do.

They all had half eaten apples which was a shame,
Where did they come from – who was to blame?
I was the innocent one – I didn't have an apple you see,
The nurse felt it must be Derek and I didn't disagree.
The patients were all marched down to the dining room for punishment,
To stand still with hands on heads until the nurse did relent.

Meantime the cottage mother came to have a chat with me,
She said "Terry, I know you couldn't be blamed for this situation.
As you had no apple this is taken into consideration."
She went round the two wards and stripped off the bedclothes on to the floor,
She smiled and said "Make all the beds up Terry, you know how it's done,
I know you wouldn't want to miss out on the fun.

It will be nice for the boys to come back to their beds made up and fresh,
And know that you supported them in this unfortunate mess."
The cottage mother guessed I was the leader of this plot,
And wanted to me to share in the punishment all the other's had got.
I admit I enjoyed this scrump and planning it all out,
Would I do it again? Yes, would the other's? that's their shout.

74 He Gave His All

He sat at the bedside holding her hand with a warm grip,
He spoke gently, lovingly, putting in the occasional funny quip.
Mary was twenty three, four months ago she lost her eyesight,
In a car accident in which she was in the right.
Her battered body was slowly on the mend.
Her depression was deep, not a smile did she send.

Peter was her lover and very best friend,
Desperately wanted to marry her so their hearts would evermore blend.
When Peter thought they were both relaxed, he moved onto one knee,
He said "Mary my love, please do me the honour and marry me."
Mary sighed "Peter I would, I love you dearly you know that,
Now I am blind my answer is no, and that is firm and flat.

If I had my eyesight I would marry you straight away,
In my condition I do not wish ever to have my wedding day.
There is no appeal to me to become a bride,
I would not be a good wife or mother however hard I tried.
Unless I ever see again I don't want to be a wife,
I am afraid Peter you must forget me and plan out a new life.

Peter was shattered, stood up, and kissed Mary goodbye,
He was not going to change her mind however hard he did try,
Six weeks later Mary as offered a transplant of a new pair of eyes,
Four weeks later she could see --- miraculous surprise.
Four weeks later Peter visited Mary, now back at home,
Her Mum and Dad went out so they could be alone.

Peter was blind, but he went on bended knee again.
"Darling Mary, please marry me, being without you is driving me insane.
You said if you could ever see again you would marry me,
Darling Mary, marry me, and we will be as happy as can be."
Mary shuddered. She could not be shackled to a blind man,
She said "Sorry Peter, I can't, you being blind, I hope you understand.

I am still young, I want to see the world and roam free,
I cannot do that with a blind man beside me."
Peter went home shattered to his very core,
He felt life was not worth living anymore,
He sent this note to Mary the very next day.
Dear Mary, Goodbye my love I will now keep out of your way.
I gave you my eyes thinking I would win your heart,
Now you have decided we must forever part.
My love for you was so strong, I loved you so,
Your refusal to marry me was a terrible blow.
With my eyes I hope the beautiful world out there you will see,
Occasionally in my world of darkness you will think of me.

I must start my life all over again, overcome my disability,
Searching for a true love who will return my love with companionship and tranquillity.

Addendum

The moral of this sad story tells you how our brain works when our status changes. Only a very few will remember what life was like before, and who stood and supported them in these difficult situations.
Our brain seeks the best way forward for the future, not caring for those who gave them sustenance and love and care in the past.

75 Singing In The Rain

I tune up with a song in my heart,
When entering the rain my song will start.
My feet itches to be out of the front door,
When out in the summer rain my spirit will soar.

I feel I am in heaven with my feet on the floor,
When I sing the songs I truly adore.
I keep my brolly up to keep me dry,
I don't always succeed, at least I do try.

I am singing in the rain with my dancing feet,
I feel so happy, free, my life is now complete.
I glide, I swirl and twirl, the occasional hop,
I dance to the rhythm that flows through me non-stop.

I dance down to the beach, on the sand by the sea,
The gentle ebb and flow is a joy to me.
I dance through the countryside and its beautiful trees,
Often I am accompanied with a welcoming breeze.

When I am dancing and singing in the rain I feel so good,
Why? I don't know why and if I should.
Come and join me to sing and dance in the rain,
Come aboard and join me on my happiness train.

When the rain stops what do I do?
I dance back home and take off a very wet shoe.
I am singing in the rain,
I am singing in the rain.

Excuse me, I hear rain on my windowpane,
My itching feet tell me it is time to dance again.

76 A Single Rose

I remember the wonderful gift of a single rose,
Presented to me when my lover on bended knee did propose.
I remember in his arms I shared the night,
With the coming of the dawn, I was exhilarated, happy with delight.

My spirit roamed high and free,
Everything was marvellous that I could see.
Oh to be in love and to be loved too,
I was in heaven, nothing else would ever do.

77 A Little Reminder

He is the one I love to kiss,
He is the one who gives me bliss.
He is the one who holds my hand,
He is the one who makes me feel grand.
He is the one I dream and pray for,
He is the one I simply love and adore.
He is the one I want to wed,
He is the one I want in my bed.
He is the one I pray will not break my heart,
He is the one I pray that we shall never part.
He is the one who I dream of the night through,
He is the one I know I love true.
He is the one I must now give a gentle shove,
He is the one I must remind he has my eternal love.
He is the one I now ask to buy our wedding ring,
So together in joy and harmony our hearts will for evermore sing.
A young lady in love cannot wait forever,
She wants the token that binds them together.

The four- twenty train to Paddington Station was late,
Passengers with connections were getting in a state
Why was the Great Western behind on time?
The serious delay was caused by 'Cow on line.'
       O-----O-----O
Susie loved to play hop, skip and jump,
Occasionally she slipped, came down with a bump.
Would get up and massage her rump,
Would always smile, never moan or grump.
       O-----O-----O
What's over the hills far away and yonder?
Because I am in a wheelchair I can only wonder.
I dream one day I will learn to fly,
To see the wide world before I die.
       O-----O-----O
We are going to the shops today,
I am going because I have no say.
I love the shops that have a seat at the door,
While my love browses all day on the shop floor.
       O-----O-----O
The idea came to me in a dream,
So clever and simple it did seem.
However in the daylight when I tried it out,
It turned out useless, no element of doubt.
       O-----O-----O
The butterfly blossoms into a vision of delight,
She will only live a day in the sunlight,
She must flitter and flutter with delicacy and speed,
To lay her seed so her next generation will succeed.
       O-----O-----O

The oak tree on our village green, always a sight to behold,
Through the season its changing beauty does unfold.
The majesty of our old oak tree is a wonder to see,
The oak has always been part of England's great history.
       O-----O-----O

Every day I drive through the beautiful countryside of Kent,
It's green field, its orchards, its valleys are heaven sent.
The government is planning with its usual bureaucratic bungle,
To turn our Garden of England into a concrete jungle.

O-----O-----O

79 Blackberry Picking

Mary went picking for blackberries, hard to find,
Because of a dry summer it was a bind.
In half a day of picking she had only filled a small jar,
To acquire this small amount she had travelled quite far.

Midday she had rested and relaxed on a style,
She was dispirited, sat thinking awhile,
Wondering where next she should go,
On to another barren patch would be a blow.

When she stood up to pursue her quest,
A fairy appeared and said "For juicy blackberries go west.
Go to Farmer Jacks farm, then down the hill,
At the bottom there is a gurgling rill.

Cross the bridge, enter the small wood,
In there are blackberries a plenty, luscious and good."
The fairy vanished as quickly as she had come,
Mary went to the wood and saw there was much picking to be done.

In the next few days Mary often visited this favoured spot,
Picked many, many blackberries for her jam pot.
Never before had she had such a good crop as this,
Mary was going to cook these berries into edible bliss.

She would make syrup and jelly and blackberry jam too,
She would have plenty over and she knew what to do.
She shared her delights with neighbours close by,
Some were returned by way of a baked pie.

Mary was not going to forget the fairy who
Helped to find these blackberries and where they grew.
She took a pot of jelly, placed it where the fairy did appear,
Thus thanking the fairy for bringing this cheer.

There is a little moral here for all to see,
Always thank those who look after you and me.

80 The Maid Wants A Rise

The housewife was upset, the maid had just asked for a rise,
Only been employed a short time so that was a surprise.
The wife said "Maria, why do you want a pay increase,
If you do not have a good reason your employment here will cease."

The maid replied "Three good reasons I will give you,
I iron better than you, obvious and true."
The wife said "Who told you that?"
The maid said "You did husband did "quite pat"

Reason two; "I am a better cook than you,
I can cook anything and don't get in a stew."
The angry housewife said "Who informed you of this?"
The maid replied "Your husband did, he said my cooking was bliss."

The third reason "I am better in bed than you,"
The furious housewife shouted "did my husband tell you that too?"
The maid replied "No, on that thought do not dwell,
It was the gardener who thought I was better than you, thought I was swell."
You will not have to think hard to get an answer or guess,
The maid's request for a rise as a complete success.

81 Birds

I look into the blue sky, there is nothing to see,
Such an absence of life is foreign to me.
Then a large flock of starlings appear from nowhere,
In unison they twist, they twirl, they spin together without care.

A thousand birds fly as one, how can that be,
Flying together, happy and free.
As quickly as they come, they swiftly fly away,
I look forward to seeing them again another day.

The Canadian Geese fly in 'V' formation,
Flying in this order they fly to distant destinations.
How did they learn to fly this way begs your consideration,
These wonderful birds always commanded our admiration.

Wait, I see a speck high in the sky.
As it comes closer a lark do I espy.
Why does this small bird fly so high?
To escape the birds of prey,
Otherwise he would die.

In the evenings the swallows put up a brave show,
Flying at speed, flying high and flying low.
Mouths wide open, into their mouths thousands of midges flow.
Swallows are very active birds, always on the go.

Look carefully into the sky and the trees,
Look on the seashore, look on the high seas.
Such a galaxy of birds that thrill and give you pleasure.
Twitchers watch for hours enjoying their leisure.

Remember birds are an important part of this world of ours,
Admire and respect their beauty, grace, agility and flying powers.

82 Blessed Peace

Peace, peace, peace,
The killing and our terrible war has ceased.
Now we can walk along the road,
Not expecting a bomb to explode.
Our water supply is slowly coming back on,
An hour in the morning and an hour at sundown.

The electricity supply will commence next week,
Limited, is the only target they can meet.
We queue at the store for our daily food,
What we get is basic and crude.
It is a meagre, we are not sure there will be any tomorrow,
Just to compound our misery and sorrow.

For six months our children have not been to school,
It will be another six months before our children respect the teacher's rule.
My brother and father are missing, we know not where,
My family and I are in constant despair.
War is so cruel, rarely is it fair,
We strive to find them alive to placate our nightmare.

We have heard nothing for months, since the end of the war,
Are they dead, injured or taken as prisoners of war.
I have scoured the hospitals, and the graveyards,
I study the army missing lists, disappointing and hard.
The basics and comforts of life will slowly return,
Our loss of loved ones will forever make our hearts burn.

Life must carry on, we live day by day,
Praying for good news and happiness to come our way.
If there are any Gods up there,
Please, please, please make the peace come here to stay.

This poem was written after reading how the Palestinians are surviving after
their conflicts with Israel.

83 A Lost Friend

Tonight as I lay down my weary head,
It is with a sad heart I go to bed.
Today I killed by accident a little friend of mine,
I was so upset I could not sit down to dine.
When cutting the long grass with my mower today,
It was then my little friend I did slay.

The monitor stalled, then rumbled to a stop,
To find the fault on my knee I did drop.
Caught in the blades my little friend Mickey the Hedgehog lay dead,
The sharp razor like blades had cut off his head.
About five years ago, the winter was cold and bitter,
Mickey, I called him, had strayed from his litter.

He was lost, alone, no mum to care for him,
In this state his future to say was rather dim.
I took him in, gave him bread and milk warmed up,
Within days he knew when it was time to sup.
Come the spring, I moved him into my garden shed,
Leaving him the choice of staying, or seeking another bed.

He soon departed into the world, making his own way,
Perhaps to find his family where he could nuzzle and play.
When autumn came and I was putting my garden to bed,
Mickey the hedgehog returned to my garden shed.
I provided a small cloth to keep him warm,
Closed the garden door to keep him from harm.

Left him water, raisins and some birdseed,
If he awakes from his winter sleep, he could feed.
This became a ritual for the next few years,
I knew it had to end sometime, it still brought me tears.
When I see a hedgehog shuffling along seeking a grub,
I am always reminded of Mickey, and my heart strings tug.

84 I Want To Touch the Sky

I want to touch the sky,
I want to swim the sea,
I want to stride over mountains high,
I want to dance in the wind, feel free.

I want to explore caverns in the earth below,
I want to cascade down the Niagara Falls,
I want to sit on the icebergs as they flow,
I want to see the sea crashing like thunderous cannon balls.

I want to see a volcano spewing its lava everywhere,
I want to spin in the vortex of a raging typhoon,
I want to see a tsunami, its fury non can compare,
I want to relax and rest in the comfort of a new moon.

I want to see the glory and colour of the setting sun,
I want to marvel when it rises to start our new day.
I want to thrill to our springtime when our new life has begun,
I want to wallow in the wonders of this world, come what may.

Some wonders of the world are either good or bad,
They are to be endured or to be enjoyed.
They are with us whether they create happiness, or make us sad,
We must respect them all if the human race is not to be destroyed.

85 It Is Wrong To Be Right

I read in the paper, again and again,
What I read is disturbing and profane.
There is so much evil in the world today,
We must all fight it our lords and masters say.
We must all do our duty, we must be good,
Stand up to the teenagers with knife and hood.
If you see a vandal doing wrong on the street,
You should gently admonish, offer him a sweet!

If lucky you will receive a mouthful expletive,
You quickly realise he is not going to be cooperative.
If they are in the mood, they will stab you in the back,
The wise retreat quickly to get out of this attack.
If you think the hoodie is unarmed, be sure, have no doubt,
You march them down to the police station, despite his shout.
You explain to the officer what this offender has done,
You relax, your good action over, good over evil has been done.

The police officer may take notes of what you say,
But beware you are in for a hell of a day.
The offender has lodged a complaint against you,
For kidnap, harassment, embarrassing him, which you should not do?
The officer will now issue you with a caution,
The offender has lied with many a distortion.
But you did take him firmly down to the station,
You are now filled with horror not elation.

The officer is pleased in his own quiet way,
He has caught another criminal he is pleased to say.
His target to catch criminals will be increased by one,
He did not have to go out in the rain or wet – what fun.
On the radio the other day I heard the pundits say,
Members of the public do not help neighbours or friend when in trouble,
they stay far away.
In the good old days, not so long ago.
When we saw anyone in trouble to their aid we would go.

If you see a child, lost, alone, walking in the street,
If you offer to help, beware the police might say you are there to maltreat.
Your good intentions are not respected anymore,
The police need you to be guilty to make up their criminal score.
The man in the street, the law, the legal system and the police, he does not
trust.
If you protect yourself or home, it's you the victim who can bite the dust.
The man in the street must at all times tread very carefully,
When defending his rights and the good, he risks getting a criminal record for
eternity.

86 If Music Be The Food Of Love Play On

If music be the food of love, play on,
Music lifts my spirit, puts me on song,
I adore music when it is full of gentle harmony,
I comfort in dreaming of love and matrimony.

I respond to the rhythm of the music of the dance,
With my partner I thrill when we twirl and prance.
When the occasion demands for solitude and remembrance,
Music can console and offer comfort to the stricken, their lives enhance.

I walk with pride when I hear the beat of a stirring march,
I visualise conquering armies walking through the victors arch.
Gentle music helps to soothe the savage breast,
Lively music can give one fire, inspiration and zest.

For many people music is their life, work and play,
They write and play music to give the world a happy day.
Music can be played to suit any occasion,
For reflexions, contemplation, celebrations, exultation and relaxation.

The world's heartbeat responds to music, fast or slow,
It soothes the weary, inspires the "Get up and go."
I cannot imagine our world without music in its heart,
It is with us from the day we are born, till the day we depart.

87 Kindness

Wouldn't it be great if we were all born kind,
We loved and cared for each other, all of the same mind.
Wouldn't it be wonderful if we all gave a helping hand?
When we saw someone in trouble, wouldn't it be grand.

Wouldn't it be kind when we saw someone ill?
We could give them a medicinal curing pill.
Wouldn't it be fantastic if we could avoid war?
We would prevent them with caring jaw-jaw.

Wouldn't it be marvellous if we could all hold hands and think?
How to stop the world from going over the brink,
Destroying itself and into the abyss of hell sink.
Wouldn't it be harmony when boy and girl fall in love?
Marry for ever, and be happy as a turtle dove.

Wouldn't it be splendid if we could play and race together?
Win or lose, remain great friends forever.
Wouldn't it be great if we were all born kind?
We loved and cared for each other and were all of the same mind.

88   A Beautiful Rose

When I look at a beautiful rose I always think of you,
You have been my love for fifty years, without you what should I do?
You are my nurse, my partner, my adoring wife,
You have been my inspiration to enjoying a wonderful life.

When the rose leaves wither and fall to the ground,
I realise the depths of our long love are strong and sound.
We are both in the final phase of our life on this blessed earth,
Let's hold hands and enjoy the rest for all we are worth.

Thank you "Dear Love" for being a wonderful wife to me,
We have had our ups and downs, had a great family.
I hope our children will find partners, who will love as we did,
Forever more to love and stay content and wedded.

89   Bleep, Bleep, Bleep

Bleep, bleep, bleep, it was the middle of the night,
Was it a fire alarm, it gave us a fright.
I dashed downstairs, was it a fire alarm?
Or a faulty gadget I could disarm?
Then the bleep, bleep, came to a stop,
Couldn't find the culprit, back into bed I did hop.

Five minutes later, it was the middle of the night,
Thank goodness there wasn't a fire in sight.
I looked out the window, what did I see?
My neighbour, half naked, fiddling with a key.
Trying to stop his car bleeping – a relief for me.
There was no problems of bleep, bleep concerning me.

I bet my neighbour with only a towel around his waist,
Thought – bloody car – and went back to bed in all haste.

90 Birds In The Summer

The summer has arrived, the birds have made or claimed their nests,
To bring up their offspring is now the acid test.
Four chicks with an enormous appetite,
The energy and food needed to feed them would give any human a fright!

To seek worms, snails, insects, berries and seed,
Depending on the season to satisfy their need.
Birds lay their eggs at a certain time,
Depending on the weather and local clime.

Knowing insects larvae thrive in the early spring,
Our feathered friends depend on them to feed their offspring.
The fledgling gorge and grow at an enormous rate,
The success of this feeding by the parents will decide their fate.

In two months' time the chicks will spread their wing,
They want to flee the nest and do their own thing,
The parents must show them how to find food and drink,
To be wary and watch for predators they must always think.

The summer has nearly come to its end,
The young birds for themselves now must fend.
They may fly off to lands far away,
Or in the land they were born they may stay.

Another family of birds, successfully brought into this world,
They must quickly learn its mysteries and how they are unfurled.
They must endeavour to remain in their prime,
To enjoy this precious life whilst they still have time.

91 Do All The Good You Can

In life,
Do all the good you can,
In all the ways you can.
Forgive and love the best you can,
To all the world in every way you can.
Praise and encourage whenever you can,
And you will never be a lonely or unhappy man.

92 A Second Chance

If we had a second chance,
To live our lives again,
To rectify the wrongs we made,
Not giving love to our dear ones,
Creating hate and strain.
If we had thought more of them than oneself,
Listened to them with love and moved their way,
Gave them comfort in their hour of need,
Happiness and joy to all would have come to stay.
The past is past, maybe for you it is too late,
To heal the wrongs to which you can relate.
Why not pass on your experience to those who will listen to you,
So in their lifetime they will not make the same mistake.

93 The Power Of Love

Generosity is love when one is giving,
Mercy is forgiveness when one is sinning,
Hope is love and support when one is expecting.
Patience is love when one endures waiting,
Bonding is the joy of loving and understanding.
Faith is the love of infinite believing.
Sacrifice is love giving all and not receiving.
Tolerance is love, waiting, forgiving and believing.
This world would be a happier place if we all could be more loving.

94 Do Not Cry For Me

You can despair for the death of me,
You can smile as from agony and pain I am now free.
You have our memories that made our hearts glow.
Your dreams tell you that I will return,
You must awake my love, I am only ash in your urn.
Your spirit one day will join me in heaven and sky,
You will grasp my hand and together we will joyously fly.
You can turn back in anguish for the morrow,
You must live for today, the future, and relinquish your sorrow.
You love me then please do what I ask you to do,
Smile, laugh, help and love others that will make the world happy and bless
you too.

95 Enjoy The Rest Of Your Life

Someday, somewhere, somehow death will visit us all,
Whether it is your turn or a friend or loved one it does befall.
The dear departed will not want you to despair for them,
Bury them with respect and when you pay your last amen,
Think of your loved ones, friends, and the world outside,
Let them remember how you overcame your sadness with pride.
That you wore a smile, gave your love, and helped others to become happy too.
Think positive and enjoy the rest of your life left to you.

96 Have We Been There Before, I Think Not?

A group of forty year old buddies did regularly meet,
Their get together was always a great treat.
They agreed to meet and dine at the hotel Ocean View,
Because the waitress were very young and pretty too.

Ten years later they decided to meet and dine at the hotel Ocean View,
Theses fifty year olds fancied the good wine list and menu.
Ten years later they decided to visit the Hotel Ocean View again,
Theses sixty year olds were unanimous in their decision and refrain.

They were appreciative of the beautiful beaches and sea view,
They joined in the entertainment and sang the songs they knew.
Ten years later now all were seventy year old,
Again they visited the hotel Ocean View we are told,

The hotel had good wheelchair accessibility,
A lift catering for everyone's disability.
At eighty years old they elected to visit the hotel Ocean View,
As they had never been there before it was somewhere new.

97 Going Home, Going Home

Going home, going home,
What joy to be going home?
Quietly I go through and close the door,
Problems and sickness are no more.

I know there will be happiness up there for me,
I am blind, but in heaven I will see.
The Good Lord and friends will bade me welcome,
A new era of my being will have begun.

My weary life on Earth is done,
I look forward to peace and the warm sun.
Fear and grief are behind me now,
I have waited long for this journey the Lord to me endow.

I am going home, I am going home,
Holding his hand my travel will be short,
It is happening, not just a wondrous thought.
The past is gone, my battles have all been fought.

Goodbye dear friends, loved ones and good earth,
I look forward to my rebirth.
I am going home,
I am going home.

98 The Master's Touch

The auctioneer stood bemused at what was in his hand,
It was an old violin, damaged, scarred, it did not look grand.
To auction it did not look worthwhile,
But the auctioneer proceeded with a smile.

"What am I bid for this interesting old violin,"
One of the audience shouted "One dollar" with a grin.
A call from the back shouted "Two" it rose to three,
"Come on" said the auctioneer "Stop teasing me."

Then up walked an elderly grey haired gentleman,
He looked tattered – like the violin – one of life's also-ran.
He lovingly dusted the old violin, tightened up the strings,
He played music as sweet as an angel sings.

The audience was dumb-founded, they clapped and cheered,
Appreciating the old man with his grey hair and beard.
The auctioneer spoke now in a voice rather low,
Respecting now in his hand was a magical violin,
Now the auction could flow.

"Who will bid a thousand dollars for this violin,"
"I will" shouted a bidder above the din.
"Who will bid me two" it jumped up to four,
It was sold for five thousand dollars, the auctioneer couldn't get any more.

The audience cheered and clapped and could not understand,
What changed its worth?
The auctioneer said "It was the touch of the master's hand."
Many a man out of tune with life,
Battered by storm, trouble and strife.

Many a good man down and out without sin,
Is discarded just like this old violin.
He travels on, moves into the slums of the city,
He becomes a vagrant, shunned without pity.

What the world does not try to understand,
We all lose so much because we do not value the touch of the old master's
hand.

99 He Was So Positive

He was positive so he thought,
Always knocked the price down on anything he bought.
Always fought to the bitter end,
Didn't care if he had to offend.
Always looked trouble straight in the eye,
The man who backed away was always the other guy.

He always walked tall with a determined face,
To lose or retreat he regarded a disgrace.
He did things his way, no deviation until,
He met a young and gregarious lady called Jill.
He became like putty in her hand,
Doing anything for her made him feel grand.

His attitude to life, being arrogant, dominant and selfish changed,
His love for Jill was so intense, some thought he was deranged.
The world was a better world now he was smitten with Jill,
Let's hope it stays that way for ever or until?!?

A frail old man was invited to live with his son,
His wife and their son thought it would be fun.
The old man was in a sad and sorry state,
His hands trembled, his eyesight blurred, they did not co-ordinate.
The family ate together on the dining room table,
To eat normally Granddad was not able.
He spilt his soup, dropped food onto the floor,
It became so bad the family could not stand it anymore.

He son said "Dads messy eating we can no longer tolerate,
What we must do now we must debate."
It was decided Granddad should sit on his own,
Make his mess on the kitchen floor which they could condone.
They knew this made Granddad sad and he cried a bit.
No one to talk to as all alone he did sit.
Then he broke some crockery, a plate and a soup bowl too,
This made his son crosser he did not know what to do.

Then his wife thought of an idea what they thought was great.
They bought Granddad a large wooden soup bowl and plate.
This made our Granddad feel unwanted; life was becoming lonely and grim.
Was this what the world, his son, his wife, their child thought of him?
All his life he had cared for others, gave of his best,
He felt to his family he had become no more than a pest.
After a fortnight of this situation had passed by,
An event occurred, so heart rendering it made Mum and Dad both cry.

Dad saw his son playing with wooden bits on the floor,
Dad asked the youngster "What are you making, what is it for?"
The little boy replied "I am making a wooden bowl and plate for my Mum and Dad,
So when they grow old of these they will be glad."
Mum and Dad knew instantly what they had been doing wrong,
The road of disrespect and non- caring that they had travelled on.
They took Granddad's hand and pressed it close to their heart,
His forgiveness they wanted him to impart.

They had realised they too would become old and grey,
Lose control of their faculties and have little to say.
Granddad sat at their table for the rest of his life,
On the table they placed a picture of his dear beloved wife.
So he could remember the days of not so long ago,
When he was blessed with good health which now was not so.
He was now happy to be part of the family again,
He had his family's love and respect, he felt he was enjoying life again.

The Moral

The moral of this story is plan for all to see,
Treat the elderly and the infirm with love and respect you must all agree,
Father Time is there watching us grow old and our youth flee,
That we all must support each other whatever our age is the key.
The wooden bowl sometime in our life could be placed in front of us,
If no one cared or loved us we would have to accept without fuss.
Some nations respect their old and treat them reverently,
We must learn to do that so we can go into old age happily.

101. I Love To Walk

I love to walk where few have walked before,
The quiet and lonely beach, with broken rocks, the ragged shore.
To view the sea, that's always in command,
It benefits Mother Nature and men's constant demand.
To amble along the freshly washed and virgin sand,
The sun smiling, the wind resting and gentle, isn't nature grand?
The gentle murmur of the distant waves is all one can hear.
A few hours later the incoming tide will appear.
The ocean is gentle, soothing, coaxing when Mother Nature is in good vein,
When upset she hurls ferocious waves, thunderstorms and driving rain.
Not the time even with sou'wester to go walkabout,
Safer to stay at home beside a glowing fire no doubt.

I love to walk where few have walked before,
In England's green and pleasant land that I adore.
The countryside in all seasons has much to be admired and seen,
In spring the bold venture forth in faint sunshine, sharp air and temperature keen.
Wander through lanes where only evergreens add to the colour flow,
In your experience and heart you know this isn't so.
You look for the young shoots bursting through the hardened earth,
Fighting to be first and seen for all their worth.
In the front line with others thrust the snowdrops small and bright,
After Winter's gloom they are a most welcome sight.
You admire the farmer's work in ploughed field and bustling farm,
These fine yeomen of England husband their produce every year without qualm.

I love to walk where few have walked before
Rambling, browsing in the Summer sun, who could ask for more.
The resurgence of Spring has clothed earth with leaf and flower,
Now the summer sun and rain will the Autumn harvest endow.
I follow the bubbling stream through wood and valley,
On the river bank under shaded tree I reflect and dally.
White clouds reflect the sun's life giving light and beam.
Enhancing the beauty of many a country side's idyllic scene.
Now is the time for the animal kingdom to graze, eat and grow fat,
Strolling through the leas and meadows give evidence of that.
The joy of a gentle and pleasant summer passes much too soon,
A benevolent summer to all the world is a cherished boon.

I love to walk where few have walked before,
Visit the orchards where fruit ripens in quantities galore.
To wander round the cornfields of barley, rye and wheat,
Standing side by side with root crops without which the harvest would not be complete.
Stroll through the avenues of our beautiful trees,
Sporting autumn colours with their tinted and shedding leaves.
The chill of the air is beginning to make its mark,
The days draw in, the evenings lengthen and it quickly becomes dark.
The nostril picks up the smell and tang of bonfire smoke,
Made by Guy Fawkes supporters and the garden fires of country folk.
On the ground one picks up the fruit of the chestnut and beech tree,
In the lanes and by- ways wild berries to be picked range free.

Venturing into the cold winter climate, make sure you close the door.
The animals in their wisdom take their seasonal sleep.
Others avoid the inclement weather and in their dens do keep.
The native birds now sing less who remain in this country now cold and grey,
Like us all sit out the winter waiting for the welcome spring day.
When the snow falls and lies crisply on the ground,
Stride out and see what winter treasures can be found.
See the frozen pond glitter in the evening sun,
Admire the children skate and slide, making their own fun.
Winter's here, enjoy it, the good and bad, come what may,
At lease we all know it is not here to stay.

I love to walk where few have walked before,
Whatever the time or season, I will find a scene that I will adore.
Mother Nature is truly beautiful, of that you can be sure,
Respect her and she will in turn reward you ever more.

102. Dad Please...

Dad please walk a little slower,
I cannot keep up with you,
You are taller, I am smaller,
And my legs are shorter too.
I follow in your footsteps best I can,
I must keep up in case I get lost.
I am only a boy, you are a man.
I don't want to be left behind at any cost.
Dear Dad I love to go walking with you,
I love it when you hold my hand,
Please walk a little slower whatever you do,
Being with you I feel happy and grand,
Please walk a little slower, I am sure you understand.

This poem you will see will encourage you to smile, thank and praise.

103. Thank You And Well Done

This world needs more productivity and more happiness as well,
This could be achieved easily, without cost if you heed what I tell.
Let us start with work, important to us all,
Most of us are at someone's beck and call.
If you have staff, you need them to give of their best,
To be one hundred per cent efficiency is the acid test.

People when happy will enjoy working for you,
Let us hope your relationship with your boss is happy too.
How to make them happy enjoy working for you,
Smile, thank and praise is genuine and true.
If you must criticise, find something to praise first,
Then lay down the law as you have to.

I'm not teaching you just be become a nice guy,
In due course it will increase your productivity, why not give it a try?
Staff who are happy, from work do not keep going off sick,
Or behind your back, sneer and give you stick.
Loyalty follows happiness, not bitterness or resent,
Giving everyone a smile, a praise, a thank you, is giving yourself a present.

Now let's look at what a smile, a kiss, praise and a thank you for your family will do.
The harassed housewife with family and home and other problems too.
To encourage her needs a kiss, praise and a great big thank you.
You might even get more bed comfort and some cookies too.
When Dad comes home after a hard day's work,
A kiss, a smile, a thank you and his depressed spirits will perk.

Win your neighbour's hearts with a smile and a thank you,
Everyone will be happier and they will guard your back too.
Are you beginning to see the power of a smile and a big thank you?
How it would make you happier and the world too,
How much does it cost to smile and praise?
A little effort and thought, but giving us all more halcyon days.

Why not smile at everyone when you walk down the street?
Many will smile back some will say "Hello" with a cheery greet.
Now my story is done, it is up to you and me to make this world happier,
More efficient is itself simplicity.
Sit back, relax, think and I am sure many of you will agree,
You will go out in to the world and act accordingly.
Smile, praise and say thank you,
Improve your life and others too.
Don't go back to your same old ways,
Look at everyone, smile and find something to praise.

As the author's poems are meant to be enjoyed and humorous, I enclose this
poem which might encourage all to pass on happiness and encourage
support to the rest of the world.

Enjoy your day and share it with everyone.

104. A Phone Call Away

My love and I had a quarrel only yesterday,
It was petty, neither could bow to each other's say.
We have been courting for nearly a year,
We have enjoyed happiness, we have shared a tear,
We were beginning to depend and rely on each other,
We had developed trust, mutual interest, enjoyed being a lover.
The question of marriage had not been put to the test,
Perhaps moving in together for a trial would be best.

I am rambling on as a woman in love does,
Whenever I see him my heart does buzz.
How are we going to make up, what should I do?
Don't let a quarrel fester, good advice that's true.
I am going to pick up the phone and say I am sorry,
Tell him our holiday booking has arrived, not to worry.
Wait, there is a ring, a phone call for me,
Please let it be from my love, please let it be.

I pick up the phone, try to remain cool and clear,
I hear the voice of the one I love most dear.
"Darling" he said "I am most sorry about yesterday,
Will you forgive me, if yes, can we arrange our wedding day?
Without you my love life would not be complete,
I want to be with you walking down Happiness Street.
If you agree we could look for an engagement ring."
It is once in a lifetime when a lady gets such an offering.

Of course I accepted, I was walking on air,
I was to be married to my love most fair.
Was it our little tiff that made him feel insecure?
Realising being parted he could not ensure.
We have been married for ten years now, we have a son,
Everything has been great from the day our marriage begun.
This might sound like a fairy story but it is true,
Why I should be so lucky I wish I knew.

I will always remember that phone call, a high point in my life,
When he rang me, saying sorry and making me his wife.
I was so relieved when he rang me first,
When I was dreading my love bubble was going to burst.

105. My Best Friend

The one who listens when I talk,
The one who insists on a daily walk,
Gives me comfort on a lonely day,
His love to me never does stray.
His large brown eyes and devoted attentiveness,
Ensures my enthusiastic stroking and caress.
At night time he acts as my burglar alarm,
Guarding me, seeing I come to no harm.
He enjoys his food, and mine too,
Until I have finished mine he knows it is taboo.
He is always there when I need company,
Whatever my mood, it's only him and me.
At night time he delights when I come home,
That's when he gets his most welcome bone.
After he has met me at the front door,
His excitement and pleasure he cannot contain any more.
Who else would prompt this loving monologue?
Only Chippie, my best friend and wonderful dog.

106. Butterflies

Butterflies dancing all in a row,
Darting and fluttering, making the watcher's heart glow.
Up and down, in and out of the trees,
They respond to the gentle summer's breeze.

Butterflies adorned in colour and white,
Dazzle us with their beauty in the summer light.
Into the flower and shrub they gently dip,
Collecting pollen as the nectar they sip.

Back into the air when they have had their fill,
They flutter serenely out of sight, over the hill.
When the night falls they take their rest,
At the break of day they again fly with zest.

Butterflies so delicate are a beauty to behold,
Their lives are short – they never grow old.
We welcome them each year to display their charm and grace,
We admire their beauty, their agility and gentle pace.

As they dance and glitter in the summer sun,
They are one of nature's beauties to be enjoyed by everyone.

107. I Am A Warrior

I am a warrior in the Queen's army,
I am British, that makes me as proud as proud can be.
When I enlisted I always wanted to be in the front line,
I knew one day with death I might dine.
I knew I could be maimed for life,
That is why I did not marry and have a worrying family and wife.
When on leave I return home to see my mum and dad,
To see me they are always so very glad.

I have been trained to kill, taught how to survive,
Short first, shoot straight, it increases your chances to stay alive.
At this moment I sit resting and huddled in a tent,
With minimum of light I must be content.
I have been out on duty, fighting, most of the day,
Two of our troops have been wounded I learn with dismay.
One shot in the shoulder, the other hit by shrapnel from a mime.
It will be a while before they recover and feel fine.

Men like us must depend on our comrades for total support,
Giving ourselves confidence when our battles are fought.
Our comrades become lifelong friends and guardians too,
To overcome our enemies to each other we must be true.
Harry, my best friend a fortnight ago, shot in the head, died,
It is not often but on that occasion I cried.
He has a family, whom I will visit when I get home,
There is nothing that a death of a loved one can atone.

The shelling and the bombs bang all through the night,
I roll over in my sleeping bag and turn off my small light.
Hoping to dream of my home and things that bring me delight,
So I wake up on the morning ready for another fight.
I am a warrior of the Queen's army, I like it fine.
When your warriors are defending you and are prepared to put their lives on the line,
SUPPORT US, ENCOURAGE US, CHEER US, DON'T SIT BACK AND WHINE.

108. I Believe…

Every day there is produced a theory on how the world began,
On how life forms developed into man.
It was man himself who decided he needed a God to adore,
To give a purpose to life because of death we are unsure.

When we die do we go to heaven or hell,
Or in purgatory do we stay and dwell.
Fearing the wrath of a God should encourage us to do good,
To make man live in peace as the world should.

Unfortunately this has not come to be,
Looking around the world today as anyone can see.
Wars fought in their god's name making this a hypocrisy.
Zealots fighting to the death with tremendous ferocity.

Man has ordained his own gods, some in his own image and made God law,
Demanding all others obey their deity or go to war.
I believe God, if he be, desires the world to live I peace,
Wars and tyranny must evermore cease.

There should only be one God, each nation worshipping with their own name,
But the rules of worship and love must be the same.
One God, one God for all the world to adore,
The human race to live on this good earth in peace for evermore.

Final Thought

A man's religion is thrust upon him when he is born,
Family and local church their beliefs will adorn.
If he does not accept he will be cast out and forlorn.
It takes a brave man to stand out against the local norm.
Religions in the past have been very cruel indeed,
So many still determined to dominate and impose their creed.

109. A Bottle Of Wine

The lady sat alone at the cosy restaurant table,
Looking sweet and demur as pretty ladies are able.
A gentleman sat at the bar, admired what he saw.
He wanted to meet her and know her more.
He asked the waiter to take over to her a note,
With a bottle of merlot wine, that is what he wrote.

Dear lady, you look so beautiful and alone, that is what I see,
Would you do the honour of having dinner with me?
She studied the bottle and on his note wrote back,
Kind sir, if you wish to dine with me, the following you must have in your
pack.
A limousine, a Mercedes Benz, two million pound in the bank will do,
Seven inches in your pants, if so, then I will dine with you.

He read the note with surprise, he was a little peeved,
At the content of the note he had just received.
He was still very interested to play her game,
He wrote back with bravado and without shame.
Dear lady, things are not always as you see,
I will clarify a few points and see what you think of me.

I have four Rolls Royce's, one outside the restaurant door,
I have residences around the world, numbering four.
This morning I had sixty million pounds in the bank, a portfolio to match,
I do hope my wealth comes up to scratch.
Beautiful lady looking as gorgeous as you do,
I will not cut off three inches just to please you.

After reading this note, to the waiter please hand the wine back,
It is obvious you are not the kind of woman I would wish to share my shack.

110. I Look Into His Eyes

I look into his eyes, they hold me spellbound,
He takes my hand, in love I feel forever bound.
In his presence I feel I am walking on air,
Every matter in my heart to my love I would declare.

I look into his eyes, they are gentle and kind,
They afford me comfort, happiness, peace of mind.
I have loved before but nothing as wonderful as this,
I now walk in the Garden of Eden where everything is bliss.

I look into his eyes and feel wondrously happy,
I know we are bound yet I feel excitingly free.
I look into his eyes, I feel I am such a lucky woman,
I will love and care for him as only a woman in love can.

I look into his eyes and wonder why the world cannot be like this,
Why all the problems and miseries cannot be solved with a single kiss.
At night we sleep, wrapped up in each other's arms and dream,
That our love for each other will never be dull, but always gleam.

111. I Remember The Storm

A few hundred years ago most of England was just green and pleasant countryside. Most of its people were peasants, who toiled in the fields and lived in small cottages, no facilities, a fireplace and chimney for heat and cooking. The cottage had a thatched roof, close by a river and a well-worn country road. The peasants grew their own vegetables, ate only a little meat. To survive you had to be very hardy and strong indeed.

Tonight, will be again long and cold,
The snow and ice and wind has taken hold.
Only extreme necessity would make you venture out tonight,
To stay indoors with fire and candle was right.
We fed the fire with log and kindled with care,
To guess how long the storm would last we did not dare.

Our family of four sat close to the fire for warmth and comfort,
Dad would tell us stories for our fear to abort
For three days we have remained inside,
Tempers were growing short, Mum and Dad each other were beginning to chide.
Our stock of food was almost gone and if the fire went out,
The world would only have our funerals to worry about.

Dawn came, the storm had passed, we smiled with relief,
Had escaped death by skin of our teeth.
We pushed open the cottage door and let the fresh air in,
The snow was so deep, we hardly knew where to begin.
Mum, my brother and I cleared the snow from window and path,
Then went into our vegetable garden to see what stocks were left after the storms aftermath.

The ground was not hard, we found some root crop.
Dad had trudged off to the village to shop,
Wishing to buy or barter for flour to bake, and meat for the hotpot.
Three hours later when he had arrived back,
He had limited supplies in his food sack.
He went straight off to check his animal traps,
He had caught two rabbits, found a large goose which through cold had collapsed.

Meanwhile Mum, Ted and me went to the woods to find fuel to burn,
We desperately needed wood before the nights return.
The heavy snow had brought down branches from trees,
We dragged them back, Dad chopped them up so that night we did not freeze.
We put the cooking pot on, building the fire up,
It was a grateful family that night who sat down to sup.
I will always remember the great storm and how we survived,
Ten families in our community did not have our resilience and resources and died.

112. Do It Today, Tomorrow We Die

Imagine tomorrow you are going to have a serious heart operation,
Anything you want your loved ones to know you say without hesitation.
You tell them you love them, they made your life feel so good,
You hug them strongly, console them the best you could.

But you know there will be no operation tomorrow,
You will not die, there will be no sorrow.
Why do you have to wait to let your inner most feelings flow?
Why not tell your loved ones you love them and make their hearts glow.

Giving love, giving care, giving consideration to everyone out there,
Will make you happy and the world seem warm and fair.
Be kind, be gentle, be understanding, listen to everyone,
You will be happier and your praises sung

Stand still, reflect on the many things you have always wanted to do,
Rise and do them now because Father Time will not wait for you.
Do them now while you are healthy and able,
If not, time passes and your dreams will become a bygone fable.

Tell the world today you love your friends most true,
They will respond and tell you they love you too.
When you have done this, make sure you do it every day,
Ensuring happiness and joy is with you to stay.

113. Don't Cry For Me

All my life I have had the luck of the draw,
I was born into a middle class family who were never poor.
I went to good schools where I did well,
On most subjects I was tops, very few that I could not gel.

I won a grant to a university of my choice,
There I was successful, gave plenty of voice,
I fell in love with a beautiful lass,
She spurned me, said I was not in her class.

Six years later she was sentenced for poisoning her hubby,
Wasn't I lucky she didn't marry me?
I applied for a job in a large company,
On the short list I was second you see.

The Chairman's son was first, no chance for me,
Dads always protect their sons, wouldn't you agree.
The Chairman's son was soon arrested for having drugs on him,
So a long prison sentence he would begin.

That left the way clear for me,
I thought to myself, how lucky can one be.
The Chairman's daughter took a shine to me,
I married her, a good future for me was now a certainty.

Our marriage turned out to be a great success,
Three healthy children were our heavenly bless.
When the Chairman died he left everything to my wife and I,
To get into my position in life I didn't have to try.

Today is my birthday, I am now seventy-five,
Yesterday was good, it was a great day to be alive.
Today I have been diagnosed with a tumour on the brain,
Three months to live, hopefully without much pain.

Yes, it's true, I knew there was something wrong with me,
I didn't expect death was soon going to keep me company.
I reflect, I have a wonderful wife and family,
All are as comfortably off as can be.

When I think of how in my life I have been so lucky,
Lay a flower on my coffin, but don't cry for me.

114. I Look In The Mirror

I look in the mirror and what do I see,
A middle aged woman looking for another he,
I lost my partner a month ago,
To me it was a bitter blow.

We lived together for two years or more,
Then he told me he was going to work on another shore.
He had been offered a job he could not refuse to take,
It was a difficult decision he had to make.

To my dismay he said we had to part,
Each our own lives we had to restart.
I could not believe our time of being together,
Meant nothing, now we are to part forever.

I look in the mirror and what do I see,
A middle aged woman preparing to party.
I have made up my face, practised my smile,
I know two gentlemen I wish to beguile.

I am pretty sure one of them fancies me,
Now it's a case, if he is, I am free.
I look in the mirror, it is time for me to go,
When I look in the mirror tomorrow I hope my heart,
With new love will be aglow.

115. I Am Just A Man

I like my ladies to be as feminine as can be,
To me a lady is the most important member of our society.
I feel ladies and family should be given the highest respect and priority,
I say that with great enthusiasm and sincerity.

On the physical side the female is weaker than the male,
In most aspects of life she can fly a higher sail.
I dream of ladies in delicate blouses, silk stockings and beautiful frocks,
I cringe when I see ladies in denim trousers, tight bottomed jeans, boots and
socks.

It gives me a thrill to mate with my love,
Enjoying the comfort of being with my turtle dove.
When I see the swaying figure of a shapely figure in a skirt,
My manly instincts tell me to woo and flirt.

My plea to the fair sex, please be as feminine as you can be,
I am just a man,
I will respond by being more passionate, more loving, more caring as I can.

116. Alone In The Dark

He stood alone in the dark,
He felt the future would be awesome indeed.
Why does the future appear so stark?
Why did he feel his heart would bleed?

His wife Mary had died a month ago,
It was sudden, an unexpected heart attack.
He had relied on her to make his life flow,
Now the pulse of life he did lack.

He looked back on their marriage together,
Their turmoil, tragedies, joys and shared contentment.
Their first meeting when their hearts were as light as a feather,
The loss of their two sons in the war he did bitterly resent.

He reflected on the happiness her smile and care she gave him,
He felt secure when she was around.
With no family and love, life now seemed so dim,
He was advised to think positive and a reason to live would be found.

Whilst watching T.V. he saw children in need,
Who wanted his love, comfort and care?
He was retired, fit, saw here was a reason to live and do a good deed,
He would go to Africa, and fight poverty and despair.

Two years later he was a manager in a children's home in Zambia,
Caring for one hundred children, helping to give them joy.
Everything is so different to his past life in Cumbria
His life is now dominated in supporting every girl and boy.

He knows Mary is smiling down on him giving her blessing and smile,
He is happy, contented, working to help those in need in style.

117. The Jewel In The Crown

I have always admired the jewel in the crown,
Sitting on the queen's head as she sits in her splendour and gown.
In her regalia when she opens our parliament in London town.
She does it with panache, with a smile, never a frown.
For her age and ability, her confidence her audiences always astound.
Even anti royalists acquiesce to her charm and renown.
I listen to those who try to put her royalty down,
With our present queen the critic becomes a clown.
When the jewel sits on Queen Elizabeth's head carrying out her duties all around,
It is not the jewel, it is not the crown,
That with respect makes her subjects kneel down.
It is her dignity, her graciousness, her charming manner that makes the world astound.

God Save The Queen and all her loyal subjects.

118. I Look At The Stars

I look at the stars in the dark of night,
The sky is clear, they are a splendid sight.
With a full moon, they are a sight to behold.
There is a chill in the air making it cold.
The snowflakes tumble to the ground,
They land delicately, not making a sound.

Soon our world will be covered in white,
The snow transforms our dull earth into dazzling bright.
Jack Frost will arrive and icicles will appear,
While they are hard and fresh you need not fear.
When they melt out of their way you steer.
Lakes and ponds freeze, you know winter is here.

We pray the snowfall will be gentle and light,
Creating magical scenes of heavenly delight.
I rise in the morning, everything looks fresh and clean,
A cold bright sun will make the world dazzle and gleam.
As I look out of my window I don't want to change this idyllic scene,
It is a wonderland of beauty and will forever stay in my memory and dreams.

119. You Cannot Please Everyone All The Time

Tom worked in the Post Office in the sorting room,
Processing illegible addresses going to Father Christmas or over the moon.
Then a few days before Christmas a letter arrived addressed to God on High,
Couldn't send it to him, cannot let it pass by.

Tom opened the letter, what it said hit him hard.
"God, I am eighty three, living on a state pension, my life has been marred."
Yesterday someone stole my purse, it had one hundred pounds in it,
That was all the money I had in the world, I had a fit.

Next week I had invited four friends to dinner on Christmas day,
They are poorer than me, now no money for food I can pay.
I have no family to turn to, Dear God you are my only hope,
Please help me out of this dilemma so I can cope.

Tom the postal worker was touched right to the heart,
So this message to all the other Post Office workers he did impart.
They were touched just like Tom, had a whip round,
Dug deep and raised just on ninety six pound.
This was four pound short of the old ladies request,
They felt sure the old lady could find the rest.

Using an official post office envelope they sent out the cash,
Enclosing a note signed God, saying enjoy your meal, don't indulge or be rash.
The Post Office group felt happy for doing their good deed for the day,
Three days after Christmas a letter to God on Tom's desk did lay.
Tom called his fellow workers to hear what the old lady had to say.

It read "Dear God, thank you for the wonderful gift you sent to me,
We had a wonderful dinner as from the photo enclosed you can see.
We had crackers and wine, all very enjoyable and nice,
By the way there was four pound missing, it must have been those thieving rascals who work in the Post Office."

120. Grannies Advice

It was a month before my wedding day,
We had invited granny over to stay.
Granny lived alone and a long way away.
We wanted her to be with us and celebrate my wedding day.

Granny was over eighty and considered quite wise,
One listened intently should she wish to advise.
One afternoon in the garden we both sat together,
Enjoying the lovely summer weather.

Granny said "I am sure everyone has told you,
How to keep your marriage strong and true.
Don't be annoyed if I give you my view.
I wish my mother told me what I will now tell you.

Ladies want to be loved, and to feel secure,
Because they want their love and family life to endure.
It is her charm and sex that brings a man to her wedding bed,
Keep him interested in both or you marriage could soon be dead.

A man in born to propagate the world as much as he can,
Mother Nature has given most forms of life that plan.
You attracted him, like another woman will to get her man,
Make sure you are his first love, not an also ran.

Many women think that once she has the family she desires,
Men will lose interest in sex and put out their passionate fires.
They were not built that way and if you shut that door,
Or allow it occasionally, or showing it has become a bore.

Don't be surprised if he responds to another woman's smile,
With open arms and sex she will beguile.
It the woman who attracts the man and she must keep him happy.
You can digest or forget what I have just said between you and me,

Is it time for a piece of cake and some tea?"

121. Goodbye My Love

It was ten years ago when we were wed,
I was so happy, time has literally sped.

Six months ago my love found another woman to woo,
Yes I was broken hearted, what could I do?

It was agreed our worldly goods to evenly share,
To do that physically I could not dare.

It was agreed I would go away for a short break,
Everything my love wanted he could take.

There would be no haggling, just a clean cut,
Once he left the door would be shut.

When I go back so little did he take?
Even though we had both contributed with an even stake.

He had left me with everything I needed, even more,
Except the man whom I had come to adore.

122. Mr. Nobody

You see him here, you see him there,
Be careful because he seems to get everywhere.
Some say he is a little funny man, or an elf,
You know he is around when something falls off the kitchen shelf.
You will know when he is about,
There will be mischief and confusion without doubt.
All the world knows him under one name,
They all blame Mr. Nobody, it is always the same.

We only see his shadow, never his face,
His presence is found in nearly every place.
He visits everywhere from time to time,
When to blame someone else is fine.
It must be he who comes in with muddy feet,
Leaves the front door open, wasting all our heat.
The ink spilled on our dining room table,
Only Mr. Nobody to do that was able.

When the taps are left on and the bath does over flow,
"It wasn't us mum, it was Mr. Nobody on the go."
When someone's dirty fingers soil the front door,
When someone leaves a mess on the kitchen floor.
When someone breaks a plate and does not report it,
Only the unseen Mr. Nobody's face will fit.
So many of us do not like to make a mistake,
Or for the blame of our errors to take.

To admit what we did was wrong,
"It wasn't me, it was Mr. Nobody" is a familiar song.
Mr. Nobody poor fellow, never seems to get it right,
Unwittingly he is often blamed for a fight.
Mr. Nobody is relived when the world goes to sleep,
For a few hours our errors on him we do not heap.
For all of us it is nice to have Mr. Nobody around,
We can all blame Mr. Nobody till another is found.

123. The Top Of The Hill

Some will say life is like a hill to climb,
I think about it and will try to define.
Where do we start? At the bottom of course.
When born we join the rhythm of life's force.

Our parents bring us up with tenderness and care,
Teaching us to love, when not to, and beware.
We go to school, we should study with zeal,
You are now beginning to realise life is like climbing a hill.

To succeed you must get onto life's continuous treadmill,
Life has its ups and downs, it can be pleasant or chill.
Most will remember the good times in their life,
Memory helps you to forget trouble and strife.

You are now a teenager learning to walk alone,
You want to race ahead, not delay or postpone.
The young girls demand womanhood to attract their man,
The boys want to be men and demonstrate their élan.

Up the hill of life they take their next stride,
Will they work and love in their homeland with pride.
Will their genes urge them to travel and conquer the sea,
Their spirits wishing to fly high and free.

Many of them will aspire to settle and have a family,
To ensure the future of the human race's continuity.
We continue to climb and pray we are not ill,
If we are, then climbing the hill will be harder still.

The family have grown and the children have moved away,
As we have grown old we sit still and stay.
We reminisce of how life has been with us,
Has it been smooth or filled with pain and fuss.

We are now old and have reached the top of the hill,
If you look over the top will you get a thrill?
Or will your body and soul just sit down and rest,
Because someone up there thinks for you that is the best.

We all have the hill of life to climb,
For some it will be hard, others just fine.
Whatever path fate has chosen for you,
Take life one day at a time and do the best you can do.

That is the best way to see life through,
Think positive, love and you will be loved too.
God Bless you.

124. The Waterfall

I was blessed to live in the country near a waterfall,
To see how it changed through winter to the autumn fall.
Its flow starts in the hills not far away,
In the wet seasons its waters gurgle and love to play.
Dancing over the stones singing a delightful song,
In the sunshine cascading in a joyous throng.

The strength of the stream depends on the rainfall and season,
The springs in the hills of time stutter without reason.
A hot dry summer would see our stream fade away,
Everyone in the village for rain would pray.
Without free running water reeds and cress would step in,
Joined by marsh plants and others to our chagrin.

The winter rains pour in and our ailing stream,
Revised, once more splashes and sparkles with a gleam.
In the spring when the flow is still fresh and strong,
We must clean out the reeds and cress, for here they do not belong.
Our joy is to see our stream flow free,
While we sit on its banks enjoying its company,
Under the shade of the osiers and our grand old oak tree.

125. Volunteering Can Be Good For You

In the world there are so many good causes to support,
So many people in need of help or distraught.
So many children need rescuing from the world's strife,
So much wildlife which should be given the chance of life.

So many illnesses and diseases that plague our world,
So many natural disasters at our good earth by nature are hurled.
So many people need to be rescued from the peril of the sea.
So many people falsely imprisoned, held hostage, deserve to be free.

So many elderly folk abused and not treated right,
Listing the world's problems we all share and face, I could write all night.
If you are blessed with good health and in good mind,
Think for a while, is there any way you can help the rest of mankind?

Large or small, give a donation, that's a start.
Could you, your energy and expertise impart?
Accompanied with some time, a little would do,
Whatever the cause you support it will need you.

The milk of human kindness is in us all,
When the plea for help comes, so many good people answer the call.
Have you thought, being a volunteer can be good for you?
If lonely or bored it would provide a new interest for you to do.

You would meet others and make new friends,
Your support is the encouraging message it sends.
To those in care and desperate need,
Your presence gives them hope and know the world does heed.

To be a volunteer can give you tremendous satisfaction,
Even if your support to the worlds needs is only a small fraction.
If everyone helped and supported a worthwhile cause,
We would all relax, smile with content, and enjoy a well- earned round of
applause.

126. Does He Know?

This was my forth meeting with my boyfriend,
This evening he kissed me, said he hoped he did not offend.
I kissed him back, gave him a smile,
I proceeded to charm him and beguile.

My feeling was we were good together,
I wanted to encourage him, keep him forever.
He gave me a strong kiss when we parted for the night,
I went home feeling full of delight.

That night I could not sleep,
Meditating on romance warm and deep.
Thomas was the third boyfriend I had ever had,
That we both felt love for each other made me glad.

He had a good job, that was important too,
Important to a girl when she lets her lovers woo.
This weekend we are going to a dance, I want to impress,
I will spend some of my savings on a new dress.

All young ladies I am sure will understand,
The emotions you have when you might get your man.
You smile, cajole, praise and agree where ever you can,
This is all part of Mother Nature's plan.

I calm down, now in future I will plan everything through
Dreaming of the great day when in church I say "I do."
Little does he know I feel my future is bright,
He will find it hard to resist me and become my Mr. Right.

127. Plain Jane

When I realised I was a plain Jane,
It was a shock, gave me great pain.
I took stock and looked the world in the eye,
I might not be beautiful, but I was not going to lie down and die.

I saw millions of people worse off than me,
Born into poverty, born disabled or into slavery.
I was determined to enjoy my life, and make my place in this world,
So together we happily embrace.

Then along came Harry, it seemed like a wonderful dream,
My life became complete, it was now full of sparkle and gleam.
They say beauty is in the eye of those who behold,
Beauty is fragile, you lose it as you grow old.

It is yourself, your love, your care that will shape your life,
I have what I want, to be happy and much loved wife.
As a plain Jane I just smiled, encouraged and loved my fellow man,
Never criticised, always praised when I can.

If you are a plain Jane, don't despair, go out and join in the fun,
Show you have a kind heart, don't mope, and revel in the sun.
Your warm nature will attract a partner just right for you,
Be cheerful, be friendly, be helpful, and you will attract a Mr. Right who
Will love you true.

128. The Amazing Dog

A man spots a notice on a household door,
'Talking dog for sale,' he thought he would like to know more.
He knocks, the dog owner welcomes him in,
"What can I do for you?" he says with a grin.
The inquirer asks "You have a talking dog is that true?"
The owner replies "Yes, he is in the garden, go and have a chat if you want
to."

The buyer finds the dog and says "Hello,
My word you do look like a splendid fellow.
Hear you can talk, is that really true?"
The dog replied "Yep, I will tell you what I will do,
I will give you a quick history of my life to date,
When six months old I found I could talk and relate.

The M.I.5 heard about me, trained me to be a spy.
I sat in secret meetings pretending not to pry.
Then I would be debriefed, M.I.5 were thrilled,
As their most successful spy I was billed.
Then I became bored, I wanted a change,
The continuous meetings were making me feel deranged.

I applied for a job at the Heathrow Airport,
As an undercover security guard, where I had to report,
On the suspicious characters who did not realise I could listen in,
My info meant so many crooks were caught because of their sin.
After four years I decided to rest and retire,
I was getting old, running out of energy and fire.

So I retired and am now enjoying a quiet life.
I have just had a litter of puppies with my wife."
The would be buyer was amazed at what he had heard,
To buy this dog his heart was now stirred.
"How much are you willing to sell this dog for?"
The answer was ten pounds if you take him now out of our door.

The buyer said "This dog is amazing, why is the price so low?"
The owner replied"That dog tells such fantastic stories when he is in full flow,
I have heard them all before, now is the time he must go."

129. Make Believe

My mother told me stories before I went to bed,
You will never be alone if you can 'Make believe' " she said.
It was when I became a teenager I tried this art,
In those days I did it with passion and all my heart.

If there was a young man who didn't fancy me,
I would lay back, close my eyes, I would cuddle him with glee.
If I was ever alone, and I was broody I do confess,
I would dream of my lovers touch and caress.

Comforted so, I would relax and soon fall asleep.
Loneliness was banished, my happiness was complete.
If I met a problem or task I could not solve,
Then I would call in Sherlock Holmes and try his resolve.

To be a good 'Make believer' it is best to have a positive mind,
It is only the good things in life a good make believer wants to find.
For company they would choose the cheerful and the best,
That would make their lives happy and give it zest.

Make believe can be great, as far as it does go,
Don't let it over whelm you, keep real life in tow.
I use my "Make believe" only as a last resort,
When I need cheering and comfort with my dreams and thought.

130. Notices And Signs That Give You A Laugh

On the repair shop door,
We can repair anything.
Please knock hard as the doorbell does not ring.

In a laundrette a notice above the washing machine,
Notice says "Please remove all your clothes if the light goes out to keep them clean."

If you need help to read this informative leaflet,
We can help you if you fill in the twenty line questionnaire set.

Outside a second hand shop,
We exchange anything, washing machines, bicycles, even the car wheel,
Bring your wife along and get a wonderful deal.

Spotted in a safari park a sign rather bizarre,
Elephants please stay in your car.

On a farm gate.
The farmer allows walkers to cross his field free,
But the bull will charge if he is angry.

Displayed in a London department store,
Go to our bargain basement on the top floor.

Notice in health shop window said,
"Sorry, closed for business, all staff sick in bed."

131. Always A Treat

The pride of lions lay in wait for their prey
By the river bank where animals came their thirst to allay.
All animals are wary of foliage by the waterside,
They know their predators in there will hide.

Four water buffalo and calf came down for their morning drink.
The pride attacked giving their pray no time to think.
The pride attacked according to their plan,
To separate the older, the weaker and off-spring if they can.

On this occasion the calf panicked and ran into the water,
A lion was on his back, intent on the slaughter.
Surprise, surprise, a crocodile had lain in wait,
He too was looking for a meal for his plate.

The crocodile rises from the depth, seizes the poor calf,
He wanted it all, he wasn't going to share half.
The crocodile then decided to have both calf and lion for his next meal,
He attacked the lion, with his pride behind him he wasn't coming to heel.

He slashed back at the crocodile, his lion pack giving support,
It was a rare occasion when crocodile and lion fought.
The young calf trembled not knowing its fate,
Seeing death only in its parlous state.

Surprise, surprise, what the pride of lions did not know,
They in turn were going to be attacked by a herd of buffalo.
The four terrified buffalo had raced back to their herd,
Quickly news of this attack was transferred.

The buffalo charged in, tossing up lions left and right,
Our brave lions, those who could, bolted, offering no fight.
The crocodile hearing the thunder of hooves and the snorts of angry buffalo,
Decided now was the time for him to go.

The baby buffalo, scratched and scarred, staggered to the bank,
Realising for his survival his family of buffalo he had to thank.
It isn't often a pride and a crocodile suffer defeat,
A story with this ending to me is always a treat.

132. Love And Kindness

What a different place this world would be
If love and kindness was every ones priority.
If we praised and loved all whom we touch and know,
Their responses would make us feel good and glow.

If we smiled and chattered to every one we met and did see,
It would be a happier world I think you would agree.
If we could let our thoughts of love and kindness flow free,
And different opinions would be listened to amicably.

If we could all agree to give to those in need,
We would get great satisfaction from our generous deed.
If the sick and the elderly are helped in every way,
With our smile and support they would enjoy a wonderful day.

A world full of wars and hate has nothing to gain,
Misery, poverty, carnage and heart break as the world takes the strain.
What a different world this could be,
If we could all smile, praise and agree.

Many of us are placed in a position,
To make the world a happier place with this simple decision.
Laugh and smile and the world will be happy with you,
Love and be kind and the world will love you too.

133. Two Kittens From Where?

Tina was nine years old, very ill indeed,
She was sick, feverish, could need feed.
She lay on the hospital bed, ashen white,
Eyes closed, she was in a serious plight.
The doctors monitored her heartbeat which was very weak,
They didn't think Tina would live another week.
One morning the nurses found two kittens lying on Tina's bed,
Each one nestled against Tina's hands on the bed spread.

The nurses did not move the kittens, they thought they would give Tina a little joy,
She could caress as you would a cuddly toy.
Tina did respond, her cold hands gave each kitten a gentle caress,
This was a positive sign the nurses did bless.
Next day with the kittens she began to play,
She even ate a little, it was an encouraging day.
The kittens purred, rolled about and frolicked with play,
Making her smile, was the sickness beginning to ebb away?

A week passed Tina was getting better slowly,
A wonderful change when a short time ago she was so lowly.
The kittens were there still gambolling about,
Tina encouraging with the occasional friendly shout.
The doctor was happy the threat of her life was gone,
He didn't understand how this apparent miracle was done.
On the day Tina was due to go home,
The two kittens vanished, elsewhere they had gone to roam.

Tina was disappointed; she had come to love them so,
But now they were gone, she just had to let go.
Who appeared from nowhere, thought to be two little misfits.
They cajoled Tina to fight for her life and live again,
Some cynics would think this idea would be insane.
Six months later Tina's mother received a letter,
From a mother whose daughter ten years old wasn't getting any better?

They stayed with her daughter till she had recovered,
Where they came from they never discovered.
They then vanished into thin air,
The kittens seem to be a lifesaving pair.
The moral of this story is plain to see,
If walking round the hospital you espy two kittens frolicking free,
Treat them with respect, they could be on a lifesaving spree,
They could be saving your loved ones, someday, even you or me!

134. When Love Walks In

I sit on the beach, throw a stone or two,
Into the sea, so calm and blue.
I sit alone, I feel restless, I yearn,
For my true love who will in turn.
Take me in his arms and kiss me,
That is how I dream it will be.

To tell me I will always be his,
Our lives together will be bliss.
I want him to be tall, dark and handsome,
The right man will hold my heart to ransom.
I have had a few lovers before,
None that I could love for evermore.

I know I am attractive, I work hard at that,
Keeping a good figure slim and pat.
I keep smiling offering warmth to all,
Unwelcoming response I have learnt to stall.
I must go back now and re-join life's stage I know,
Take part in the hustle and bustle of life's flow.

Waiting for the next step of my future to begin,
When my true love opens the door and walks in.

135. The Wise Man Said…

The wise man said,
The world without the woman of the street,
It would be a world that was incomplete.
Ever since man and woman dwelt on this earth,
Nature ordained that man and woman should together create birth.
Man was fashioned to provide passion and fire,
Woman was created to attract her man and satisfy his desire.

Man is ever ready to have sex at will,
Whenever available he will have his fill.
Woman uses sex to beguile and attract her man,
When courting is over, to have children is Nature's plan.
The ladies when they have had the children they desire,
Often lose interest in satisfying their partner's fire.

She still wants to be attractive and admired by all,
But sex is no longer on their stall.
Now we have a man with plenty of sex left in him,
His enjoyment in bed life has now become very dim.
He goes to find his solace with a woman of the street,
She makes him feel wanted, and his desires do meet.

With this new arrangement now in hand,
The father and husband stays as a family man.
When the men folk and soldiers travel far away,
It is the woman of the street their frustrated passions allay.
Men are designed to want to satisfy their passion all their life,
Unfortunately this is not so for many a wife.

Now let us look at prostitutes from their aspect,
Think it through and you might give them some respect.
Why do ladies often reluctantly go on "The Game?"
Many get no pleasure and are put to shame.
The hours are long, they can be seriously abused,
Many are exploited, they can be hurt and misued.

Imagine a woman with children deserted by her man,
In financial trouble, needs money as fast as she can.
She has no skills with which to earn her keep,
To become a prostitute is a tremendous leap.
She could be humiliated, were her friends to find out,
But it pays her bills and financial troubles are put to rout.

To support her family she is so keen to do,
Because she is a mother and loves her children too.
To consider this subject further, prostitution will never be gone.
So we should protect our ladies, do not let them be preyed upon.
The wise man continued,
I personally feel their profession should be given some respect,
Legalise it and banish its criminal aspect.

Many countries have made their brothels legal, all to the good,
Then it would be pointless for criminals to exploit a woman as a prostitute.
Keeping a watch on the brothels would mean we could clean up the trade,
Licence them, stop them walking the streets where they are afraid.
I accept some of society would not want their sexual habits put on show,
But the world would be a better place that I do know.

Moral attitudes in this country would have to alter to make this plan flow,
It could stop rapes, abuse of children and other crime in tow.
Powerful sexual desires in man are here to stay,
It would be beneficial if men could their passion for a woman in a brothel
allay.
It should reduce disease, crime, and produce taxes for the Inland Revenue,
The police could now direct their energies elsewhere, another benefit, that's
true.

The wise man concluded "It doesn't take much thought to reason this out,
The benefits are substantial to everyone there is no doubt."

136. He Loves Me True

My name is Mary, my boyfriend is Johnny,
We both work hard, do not earn a lot of money.
We have been going out together for nearly a year,
We both feel so content when to touch each other we are near.
We are both rather shy and do not say a lot,
I feel our love is the best thing we have got.
When we cuddle and kiss I do not feel his fire,
Even after the advice given to raise his desire.

We meet at least three times a week,
I know we are both keen, regard them as a treat,
I drop hints about our future together,
He becomes nervous, flustered, rather talk about the weather.
I know I love him, and he loves me too,
How to tie the knot, I am not sure what to do.
When a girl meets a boy she loves and is rather shy,
She must persist with her feminine charm, gently seduce, try, try, try.

Last week for a few days he was away,
To see his Grandma he went to stay.
Whilst he was there he sent me an envelope, in it a ring,
With a note, proposing to me, how my heart did sing.
He was too shy to propose to me face to face,
Later he told me if I had said no he would have felt a disgrace.
He had counselled his Grandma, whom he could trust,
She advised him strongly, we should get wed, that was a must.

Tomorrow Johnny comes back from him Grandma after a long train ride,
I will meet him at the station and be by his side.
I have arranged a quiet dinner for the two of us,
I know he would not want any fuss.
I will tell him this is the happiest time of my life,
Now I know we shall become man and wife.
I feel alive, so happy, I just can't wait till I say I do, I do, I do.
I am over whelmed he cares for me and loves me true.

137. It Didn't Seem Fair

Harry joined the army, became part of the bomb squad,
Soon realised the dangerous path he trod.
He was trained to be diligent if he wanted to survive,
To take extreme care if he wanted to remain alive.

You need Lady Luck to be on your side, that's sure,
Without her blessing you would soon be at death's door.
After twenty years Harry retired with honour and grace,
No more enemy bombs would he be blow up, dispose of or face.

His experience and courage still controlled his destiny,
His services in the commercial world were required by many.
He formed his own company, became a wealthy man,
Blowing up bombs, clearing sites, all according to his clients plan.

I stand by his grave, he died at the early age of fifty five,
If he had taken more care he would still be alive.
It wasn't a bomb that his life did end,
It wasn't Lady Luck whom he did offend.

When crossing the road he didn't take enough care,
He got run over, after all the risks he took it didn't seem fair.
Moral of this story is plain to see,
There is danger everywhere I think you will agree.
The Grim Reaper is ever ready to receive you or me,
Always take care and remain in the land of the living and free.

138. New Aspirations

Do you feel down, don't know what to do?
Cannot face the world, all seems black and blue?
Let us sit down and think of what you can do,
To help you see this miserable patch through.

They say it is all in the mind when you become like this,
And all you want is a little happiness, perhaps a kiss.
A little word of encouragement would not go amiss.
Helping to quell your sadness, creating a little bliss.

Perhaps it is you, who should make the first move,
Show others you love them, sure they will approve.
Greet them with a smile, say "I love you".
It is amazing what those few words will do.

Take their hand, smile, say sorry if you have to,
It might be hard, if you want happiness, this you must do.
Get yourself interested in the world outside,
Perhaps become a volunteer, wear that badge with pride.

Think of the millions of people worse off than yourself,
Think how lucky you are, get off the desperation shelf.
Forget about your sadness, think of others you can support,
To make them happy, it will give you a feeling of import.

Be positive, smile, go out into the big wide world, savour the sunshine,
Both you and the world together will make you and your friends feel fine.

139. Mutton Dressed As Lamb!

Yes it's true I have now turned sixty four,
Now widowed I don't get men calling at my door.
I really miss having a man by my side and in my bed,
One I can look after in our comfortable homestead.

One to call me love, give me a frequent kiss.
I would always respond and stir up his passionate fizz.
I am alone and desire a man's companionship,
When I get him I will keep him on my loving and firm grip.

I go to charity shops and I dress very well,
I buy saucy undies, I know you can't tell.
Trying to get me another man I enjoy doing you see,
It gives me a thrill in life and the excitement makes me happy.

When I smile at a prospect and he smiles back at me,
My heart thumps, will he smile, perhaps wink at me?
Will he ask my name, take me out to tea?
Will he ask me if I am free, I am, will he be?

If he does not, my experience comes into play,
I say "Hello, I hope you are having a great day."
I wait for his response and what he will say.
Be sure, I will not let him slip easily away.

I live in a small flat very near the city centre,
On the ground floor, easy for my discreet lovers to enter.
I am not ashamed to say I still want to satisfy a man,
I want him to love me as passionately as he can.

They say "I am mutton dressed as lamb",
I am a woman coming to the end of my life span.
I have enjoyed a happy life; love has always been there,
Whatever life I have left, for a lover or partner to hold my hand is my prayer.

140. Now We Must Part…

I remember when I loved you and you loved me,

The world was a heavenly place to be,

Now we can't agree or see eye to eye,

I feel so sad, I want to sit and cry.

Where and why did it all go wrong?

When we were married we sung such a happy song.

Last week our marriage is in its fifth year,

Now we never call each other darling or dear.

The last few months we have not slept together,

We both feel our marriage we should sever.

We did not marry in haste, we courted for three years,

Now we are to part with sorrow and tears.

My husband says he has found another to care for,

What hurts, I loved him so, I couldn't give him anymore.

Life goes on, yes, I want to fall in love again,

I look for love and sunshine in my life, my spirit,

Will not be overcome by life's cold and cruel rain.

141. An Unpleasant Customer

At the airlines reception desk sat a single attendant,
A very long queue of irate customers on her was dependant.
To rebook their flights which had been grounded,
Some thought for reasons totally unfounded.

Suddenly an irate customer barged his way up to the front of the queue,
His attitude and rudeness created quite a to do.
He shouted "I have to be on the next flight,
It has to be first class, I must leave tonight."

The attendant quietly said "Sorry sir, you must take your turn,
We treat all our passengers equal concern."
The customer roared "Do you have any idea who I am?"
Without any hesitation she grabbed the public address system,
So boldly said "Everyone quiet please and carefully listen,
We have a passenger at desk fourteen who does not know who he is,
Could someone identify him before he gets in a tiz?"

The folks in the queue roared with laughter, saw the bully was not going to succeed.
Our bully now was totally upset and aggrieved.

He stamped his foot, shook his fist and said "Damn you and blast",
She calmly replied "Sorry sir, but you will have to get in the queue for that too."

142. What A Surprise!!

An Irish doctor wanted to take a day off from work,
His responsibilities to his patients he was not going to shirk.
He said to Murphy, his inexperienced assistant,
If he could look after the clinic for a day, did he feel competent?

"Yes sir" Murphy replies, "You need not have any doubt,
You are on the mobile, if any problems I can give you a shout."
The doctor goes fishing, has a well- earned break.
Next day back at the clinic he asks Murphy about his day's intake.

Of patients who had needed treatment throughout the day.
Murphy was pleased with himself and had this to say.
"The first patient called in, had a headache, I gave him paracetamol",
"Bravo" said the doctor, "that follows the good doctor's protocol."

"The next patient had indigestion, I gave him Gaviscon, that I did do",
"Bravo" said the doctor, "Full marks I give you.
What about the third patient you have in your day book,
Tell me what her complaint was and the action you took?"

Murphy replied "It was mid-afternoon, all was very quiet,
From the paperwork I was taking a respite.
Then the door flies open, a gorgeous young woman rushes in,
She looked beautiful, seductive and beguiling, and without sin.

Without a word she tears off her clothes, her bra, her knickers as fast as she can,
I was lost, I could not think of any plan.
She lies down on the table, throws her legs apart,
I did not know what to do, how to start."

She screamed "Help me for the love of St. Patrick, please help me if you can.
For five years I have not enjoyed or seen any man."
The doctor gasped, "What did you do, this was a hell of a surprise?"
Murphy said with quiet calm "I simply put drops in her eyes."

143. How To Write A Short Story

The English teacher told her class to write a short story,
About religion, sex and mystery, must not be gory.
It was to contain as few words as possible,
Using only the English language was permissible.
The winner's short story was stunning you must admit.
"GOOD GOD, I AM PREGNANT, WHO COULD HAVE DONE IT?!!"

144. Pull The Other Leg

A little boy was waiting outside a grocers shop,
When a man asked him "Where was the next bus stop?"
The boy replied "Sure, straight down the street, turn right,
Two hundred yards and the bus stop will be in sight."

The man said "Thank you, I am the new vicar in town.
Why not come to my church next Sunday, love to show you around.
I will also show you how to be happy and show you how to get to heaven,
Interested?"
The boy replied "Pull the other leg, you could not even find the bus stop
unassisted."

145. I Made It

It was 1947- two years after the last Great War,
Germany was smashed, ravished and was desperately poor.
When the war was over Russia sent her Cossacks in,
They were the meanest of men and knew no sin.
The Germans had ravished Russia, raised towns to the ground,
Murdered citizens, raped any woman they found.

Millions of Russians died of the severe winter cold,
The lucky ones from German bullets we are told.
So when Peace was signed Stalin retaliated,
Ordered his soldiers to the Germans to dish out hell unabated.
It was the Russian Cossacks to this task were designated,
They in turn ravaged, raped, murdered – their ferocity was unabated.

When their fury was spent and Germany was devastated,
The world realised that Germany as a country had to be rebuilt and
reinstated.
A few small towns and villages had escaped the wrath of war,
Without the country's wealth they were extremely poor.
No trade, only their garden products and farmers' harvests they had to sell.
But salvation came, as under the British Army's occupation they had to dwell.

Once billeted, they called the town's council together,
Pointing out that they must work and unite or they would remain in this
terrible mess forever.
Interpreters from the townsfolk were called for,
Twenty-one men and women passed through the recruiting officer's door.
One was Fraulein Hilda – an attractive lass of nineteen,
To get a paid job she was very keen.

She like many felt there was no future in Germany any more,
To marry a British soldier, was the only future she saw.
The British soldiers away from home so long were hungry for love,
She was going to play it hard to get – make sure she would be someone's turtle dove.
Whether she loved him or not she didn't really care,
She was going to get to England as his wife, so there.

She was designated to an office to distribute everyday information about,
Put there because of her excellent English no doubt.
The soldiers in the office around her began to pinch and grope,
To ward off their advances she soon learnt how to cope.
She wasn't ready for a one night stand,
She was playing for a wedding ring and a wedding band.

It took a month for an offer to look her way,
She decided this was the one to play.
He visited the office twice a day,
To collect office papers and asked her for the latest information and went on his way.
She couldn't put on sexy clothes, there weren't any about,
Lipstick was like gold, so little you did without.

She had brought some old dresses – her mother shaped them to look like new,
Her only consultation – all the other girls were in the same boat – just like you.
Then her mother suggested a wheeze that might work out,
When he was in the office, twist your ankle and with pain shout.
Suggest you would appreciate it if he could take you home when office was done.
If he fancies you an opportunity like this he would not shun.

Sure enough, that is how it turned out to be,
Ted was doing the chasing, ladies we know better don't we?
Three months later they were married against the army's advice,
Nine months later they went to England as Hilda had planned to do.
She was pregnant, they both thought this was wonderful too.
She was going too England to start life anew.

It would be many years before she could bring her family over too.
Married forty years, three boys, a nice home and a loving husband,
This was all better than she planned,
When she was a Fraulein in Germany when it was down and out.
But now from its ashes it has risen and with the world as its equal,
Its flag does proudly flout.

146. Our Wonderful World

Have you heard the gurgling of a happy stream?
Have you wanted to climb to the moon on a midnight beam?

Have you marvelled at the beauty of a setting sun?
Have you thrilled at the sunrise, another day has begun?

Have you sighed at the magnificence of the ice capped mountain?
Have you mused at a multitude of birds playing in the fountain?

Have you wondered how life exists in the harsh Sahara sands?
Have you watched in amazement how spiders swing on their delicate strands?

Have you trembled when you see volcanoes erupt their lava flow?
Have you puzzled why cheetahs are so fast, tortoises so slow?

Have you thought why men's lives are so short, but the world goes on for ever?
Have you wondered why our good earth should have four seasons of different weather?

Have you deliberated why man is on this world at all?
Why all other planets in the universe never answer man's call?

147. The Alphabet Of Love

Adore
 The joy of true love is when each other they truly adore,
 Loving today and holding hands for ever more.
Beguile
 The fair sex is blessed with femininity, with charm to beguile,
 Mother Nature adds to her armoury a bewitching smile.
Courtship
 Courtship is best when it flows gently along,
 Giving each other lover time to savour the others heart felt song.
Dear
 Everyone desires to be some ones precious dear,
 It brings you love, contentment and great cheer.
Ecstasy
 When you are in love, you are in ecstasy, you can dance on air,
 The world is wonderful, you hear music everywhere.
Fiancé
 Every young woman dreams of having a fiancé in tow,
 Gives her a thrill, comfort, a boost to her ego.
Gallant
 A young lady dreams of her man, to be tall, handsome and gallant,
 To attract his attention she must use her array of feminine talent.
Heart
 When you are in love, you must open your heart,
 Let them know what joy their presence to you does not impair.
Intuition
 It is well known that a woman has more intuition than a man,
 She can assess a good partner, better than a man can.
Joy
 Love should be the occasion for great happiness and joy,
 Nature's unification to bring together girl and boy.
King
 To be successful in marriage a woman must make a man feel like a king,
 He in turn must woo her every day and make her heart sing.

Love
The world needs love, so we can all live in peace,
Enabling true love to flourish and never cease.
Marriage
Marriage should be the union of two loves becoming one,
Loving each other, supporting and caring for each other until day is done.
Nurture
If only this world could be taught to nurture love not hate,
Then this world would be heaven, not in its present unhappy state.
One
When a man and woman can love and act as one,
The fight against loneliness, sadness and misery could soon be won.
Passion
The world needs passion, passion resulting from love and good will,
Both partners to enjoy its consummation and its thrill.
Queen
When a woman is in love she should be happy as a queen,
Her beauty bursts forth, she is more lovely than she has ever been.
Ring
Is it the ring on the telephone from her love she is waiting for?
Is it a wedding ring which most ladies will adore?
Sex
Is it nature's call for sex that brings lovers together,
Make love and bring up a family to their best endeavour.
Treasure
To young and old lovers, memories are always a treasure,
Rummaging through photo albums of the past is always a pleasure.
Universe
Lovers bill and coo throughout the universe,
Love is the universal language in which we can all converse.
Vow
A wedding vow is a promise to bond forever,
During good times or bad, to always be together.

Win
 If you want your union to succeed and win,
 Be quick to bless and forgive each other their sins.
Xcite
 The joy of being together, the ability to each other excite,
 Will bring happiness and satisfaction, especially at night.
You
 The importance of love is making both lovers happy too
 You must always think first of him, and he must always think first of you.
Zest
 For a marriage or union to be blessed
 Requires hard work, patience, care and zest.

148. The Woman Of The Street

Yes, I am a woman of the street,
I satisfy men's desires I compete,
Demanding them to pay for their treat.
My regulars with a smile I always greet,
I meet their needs if on their wives they cheat,
If they can't get satisfaction under their marital bedroom sheet.
Men with family try to be discreet,
Desire to meet me in my bedroom or a quiet backstreet.
Some men want fire and their passion to delete,
Some want me to stimulate their heartbeat.
If I don't satisfy them their wives may mistreat.
Many men come to learn how to make their loving more upbeat,
Single men come to sate their passion and make life forever sweet.
Some want a thrill in the back of a car seat.
Some men just want sex and make me feel downbeat.
Most regulars come to be comforted and enjoy a happy repeat.
Men are made to propagate the world and are sexually replete,
Since the world began there has always been a need for the Woman of the street.
To satisfy the lust and desires of wanton man and make him complete.

149. The Fantasy Wife

How did I get into this position you might well ask,
When I was twenty one life took me to task.
Had two small children when my husband of aged twenty five died.
Financially I was broke, I just sat down and cried.
My husband's best friend came to my aid,
We moved in with him, all our bills he paid.
I did not know what to do, the future was not bright,
I could not see any prospects in sight.

There were no jobs about I could work at,
I had two children to look after, that was that.
Then one of my friend's friends approached me,
Asked "Once a week could he visit me?
Have sex and pay my agreed fee."
With no other prospects in sight I did gladly agree,
No other way forward did I see?
My morals in this matter did quickly flee.

When he visited he wanted more than sex I could plainly see,
He needed my love, he wanted to be wanted by me.
He desired to go back to the days of his honeymoon,
When his wife wanted him, he was ecstatic, over the moon.
Five years of married life, the rot has set in,
His love life was on the rocks, he could not win.
His wife put up with him, but not in bed,
For that comfort he came to me instead.

I realised he wanted sex and a shoulder to cry on,
I learnt quickly how to beguile and respond.
As he spent a couple of hours with me,
I of course had to double my fee.
It must have been this gentleman I am sure,
Who told others, because another came knocking at my door.
I told him for an hour or maybe two,
To make him happy, my best I would do.

I was not a whore, where he would be in and out,
Told him my terms, cash up front, so he was not in any doubt.
I made my flat and home as welcoming as can be,
Now I could afford to send my children to nursery.
I would only entertain guests between one to five,
There after my home and children had to become alive.
Some of my guests came weekly, others on a regular basis,
Luckily I rarely had vacant places.

I would write down the likes of each guest or not,
Most men wanted loving sex, and their troubles out to me trot.
I made lots of money and received presents too,
When my guests left, they were relaxed, ready to face the world anew.
In a way I felt I was providing a service to society,
Many would not say I was going against social propriety.
I enjoy what I do, that I do not deny,
Sometimes I lose out, and then I sit down and cry.

In such moments I remember what one of my guests said to me,
"You are my Fantasy Wife, I would marry you if I was free."
One of my guests was an advisor of investment accounts,
He managed my financial affairs, on my services I gave him a discount.
As fifty I plan to retire and close shop,
I dream of going around the world on a cruise non-stop.
Looking back I like to think to many I gave happiness,
My services kept families together, saving a lot of stress.

I am grateful to those ladies who let me be a Fantasy Wife,
Most of my guests come seeking happiness in their life.
They just felt they needed to be wanted,
In their family life not only just in bed.
The moral of this story is plain to see,
If you want a happy marriage, whether it be he or she,
Tell each other you love them dearly, be sincere and true,
Give yourself freely, love will bond, otherwise the future you might rue.

150. Today Will Not Come Again

My love, my love, today will not come again for you,
Now alone I must see my life through.
Now you are gone I know what I will truly miss,
Your welcoming smile, your adorable kiss.

Your encouragement when I was down and out,
I always had hope and inspiration when you were about.
My love, my love, we dreamed our love would last for ever,
Your demise our dream did surely sever.

I walk the walks that we did together,
Lovingly holding hands, whatever the weather.
With you beside me I felt happy and strong,
Our hearts to each other did belong.

My nights now are lonely and long,
With you my love I always felt part of a happy throng.
I look into the sky and see your adorable face,
My heart beats faster, I walk a quicker pace.

Your memory will always bring comfort and joy to me,
I long to be in your loving arms again, whenever that will be.
My love, my love, today will not come again for you,
My heart will always be yours, my love forever true.

151. Passion

We were married two years ago
Our original passion was fading in its flow.
I feel I must relight it again
To save our marriage coming under strain.

I haven't put on much weight since we were wed
When we make love we satisfy each other in bed
We used to make love three times a week
Now once a fortnight my loving arms he does seek.

I have decided I don't want him looking elsewhere
Falling into the arms of another woman I couldn't bear.
So I am going on the attack, changing my underwear
I want us back as a passionate pair.

I brought several pairs of saucy panties
Wanting to stir the fires with enticing scanties
Brought some bras showing plenty of cleavage
All designed to give me extra leverage.

I bought two pairs of black stockings which he admires
Now I am ready to start to kindle his fires.
I wear a shortish skirt to show a thigh
Now I want more than my man's admiring sigh.

Well my plan worked out I am pleased to say
On a Saturday night I wore my alluring array
It wasn't long before my love took me to bed
He was passionate as on the night we were wed.

Next morning I told him straight
I didn't want last night's passion to abate
I wanted him to make love to me a lot more
He realised I was serious and that was the score.
Now he does that with much pleasure I am sure.

152. I Am In Paradise

I am in Paradise,
Never give it a miss,
I am in paradise,
Introduced by a heavenly kiss.

Go there, it is simply bliss,
I discovered my Paradise when I met you.
I want to stay in paradise
Because of my love for you.

When in paradise I feel so good,
Each day comes in gloriously new.
I am in Paradise dreaming
Of our love strong and true.

I am in Paradise walking on air,
In Paradise the skies are never grey.
Nothing in life can compare,
Sunshine beams down me every day.

In Paradise with happiness I sleep,
When I touch you my heart with joy
Does bound and prance and leap.
Knowing tomorrow with you my life is complete.

In Paradise I dream of the great day
When you will bond with me and say "I do,"
Even in Paradise the wiseman say,
You both must become one, your love must always be true.

I am in Paradise with the woman of my life,
Dear Lord, for evermore please keep it that way.
You have given me a blessing, a wonderful wife,
Please help us in the land of Paradise to stay.

153. GLOBAL WARMING IS HERE.

From our glass conservatory I look out,
With the leaves falling I know autumn is about.
Autumn has come much later this year,
It is all about global warming I hear.

With the earth warming up, the seasons are in disarray,
Fortunately we are keeping the same night and day.
If the weather patterns change and we have early or late spring,
Birds with their new born chicks will be caught napping.

Insects confused by a warm winter or an early spring,
May not be available for the birds to satisfy their chicks feasting.
With the advent of global warming the world must quickly adapt,
The breeds that don't will soon disappear and that is a fact.

From our conservatory in the garden I look out,
I espy spring flowers thrusting up anxious to be about.
They are unaware that any moment Jack Frost could strike them dead,
This could happen to any shrub missing its winter sleep and bed.

Birds are still here because of the warm weather,
When to warmer climes they should have taken their feather.
The leaves on the trees are now beginning to fall,
Usually before now they are grounded I do recall.

From our conservatory window into our garden I look out,
I see the birds in the bird bath splashing about.
Like us they no longer worry about this summer's drought,
In the hot dry summer our lovely green lawn dried completely out,
Even the weeds were put to rout.

After six weeks of rain everything is lush and tall,
Reluctant to go to their winter bed at all.
The birds are grubbing the soft earth feasting on insects, having a ball.
The evening draws in, the night descends so quick,
With global warming here, I wonder what will be Mother Nature's next trick.

154. Our Wonderful Trees

Where would we be without the blessing of a tree?
Their benefits are tremendous to everyone its plain to see.
Through its leaves it cleans the air we breathe,
The more trees we have, the less we heave.
The trees on this earth have served humanity well,
Their beauty, their foliage, their changing colours cast an enchanting spell.
So many birds depend on the trees to provide nest and food,
So many animals depend on trees, in order to bring up their brood.

Where trees grow, their roots bind the crumbling earth,
Without trees arid heath lands and deserts are given birth.
Trees are noted for attracting the rain,
Keeping the earth cool and moist, another gain.
Since the world began and Mankind needed fire,
Without kindling wood in the winter, man's future would be dire.
Early man used the leaves and the branches to make a thatch
Nomadic tribes could quickly build simple huts from scratch.

As the world's civilisation of man gradually matured,
It quickly appreciated the strength of wood, it became inured.
Wood was needed to build ships of great strength
To explore the world's oceans, their breadth and length.
Thinkers of the world realise the tremendous importance and beauty of
wood
All life on this planet, know trees are vital to our existence for good.
When we walk down an avenue of trees
Stroll through a forest, admire the maturity, the beauty, as you please
Appreciate the Majesty, the diversity the durability of our wonderful trees.

When you look over our country's green and pleasant land,
You admire the fields, the valleys, the rivers, the mountains, supported by
trees most grand.
The fruits of the trees bring pleasure and nourishment to our table
Is there any other natural product on earth which is so important and
Capable.

155. Harvest Time

I remember as a country lad when I lived in the village of Little Carlton,
It was harvest time that demanded every ones attention.
All prayed the harvest would be good,
Each prayed when harvesting started then sun would shine as it should.

When it came to the cutting of the wheat, the barley and the rye,
Blue skies, bright and dry days would set our hopes on high.
The men with sickle and scythe would cut through the long day,
The woman folk would provide sustenance and support all the way.

Behind the men the ladies would bundle and stack,
The elders and children would join in and bend their back.
They brought in the wagon cart and two horses to carry the grain,
Back to the barn where throughout the winter it would remain.

The fruits of the season could be picked in a more relaxed way,
Apples, pears, berries each in turn held their sway.
Everyone joined in to glean the crops and pack them too,
To ensure they would keep in good condition the whole winter through.

It was the gathering of the harvest that kept the villagers all together,
They pulled as a united team whatever the weather.
The harvest would be the result of a hard years toil,
Sowing the seed, cultivating, extracting the most from the earths precious soil.

When it came to the Harvest Festival and the blessing in the house of the lord,
Everyone came to celebrate, give thanks, each on their own accord.
A successful harvest would make all the villagers hearts glad,
It meant in winter, food on the table, coal in the hearth, and folk well clad

Then we had three bad years when the crops were poor,
That was when poverty and disaster came knocking on our door.
We had no alternative but to look in another place,
Dad's brother ran a small factory in the Midlands that made lace.

He offered us shelter, provided mum, dad and me a job too.
We would all have to reorganise our lives and learn many things anew.
Its three years now we have lived in Buxton Town, Dad's brother has been kind,
Helped us settle in, always obliging, nothing a bind.

My family and I know we shall stay here the rest of our days,
But nothing will ever replace our happy memories of harvesting and the country ways.

156. Howzat!

It was glorious weather, the cricket match was soon to begin
To waste this lovely sunshine would be a sin.
There is some information to you I must impart
Before this battle of bat and ball is to start.
The opening batsman is the umpire's son
In front of his home crowd he wants to make his first ton.

The opening bowler is Freddie Truman of England fame
His reputation for fast bowling the cricketing fraternity do acclaim.
The scene is set, the batsman takes his guard
Batting against Fiery Freddie will be hard.
Freddie raring to go, runs thirty yards and bowls at the wicket
Batsman plays forward, misjudges, and snicks it.

First slip takes a good catch, the result is not in doubt
Freddie looks at the umpire and gives a thunderous shout.
The umpire shakes his head and says "Not out – Not out."
Freddie picks up the ball and bowls again
The batsman plays forward – plumb lbw – "Howzat" is everyone's refrain.
The umpire stands impassive – he is not giving his son out.
Negatively shakes his head – element of doubt?

Freddie's temper was now beginning to run very high
He walked back with the ball for another try.
This time he sent down an absolute corker
It was an unplayable in swinging Yorker.

It knocked the three stumps out of the ground
Triumphantly Freddie waved his fist in the air and turned around
And said to the umpire without being verbose "By gum lad, that must have been close!!"

157.How To Enjoy A Happy Marriage

Marriage is a union between a woman and a man,
Both should strive to keep it as happy as they can.
First of all no partner should the other criticize.
Praise first, gently admonish, then smile encouragingly, that's wise.

Remember to use the word "We" whenever you can,
Don't emphasize the difference between woman and man.
Both of you together must smile, smile, smile,
Of course it will help the lady to beguile.

Once a day say I love you
This must be sincere and true.
When walking together always hold each other's hand,
It will make you feel proud, content, united and grand.

Praise your partner for every meal they make,
You will get even more delicious cookies and cake.
You must both satisfy each other's sexual need,
Very important if you wish your union to succeed.

The lady should always be feminine and ready to flirt,
With her beloved partner so he is only interested in her skirt.
A kiss in the morning when you are awake,
A kiss at night before sleep you partake.

Never go to sleep with a quarrel on the boil,
Settle it now, or tomorrow it will cause misery and toil.
Share your relaxation times, you'll be as happy as can be
If you respect your partner's hobbies, whatever they may be.

The lady should always make the man feel like a king
Make sure she holds the purse and pulls the string.
You must keep each other your individual identity that's true,
But think play, plan and love together whatever you do.
Remember, a marriage is supposed to be for life,
It should be a joy, a haven, a blessing without strife.

Dear friends, thank you so much for reading my poems, I hope that they bought you lots of enjoyment.

Look out for my new book, coming soon.

Terry Godwin
The Laughing Poet

Made in the USA
Charleston, SC
11 July 2016